HOPE BEHIND BARS

HOPE BEHIND BARS

NOTES FROM INDIAN PRISONS

Edited by

SANJOY HAZARIKA

MADHURIMA DHANUKA

MACMILLAN

First published in India in 2022 by Macmillan
an imprint of Pan Macmillan Publishing India Private Limited
707 Kailash Building
26 K. G. Marg, New Delhi 110 001
www.panmacmillan.co.in

Pan Macmillan, The Smithson, 6 Briset St, Farringdon, London EC1M 5NR
Associated companies throughout the world
www.panmacmillan.com

ISBN 978-93-89104-02-8

1 3 5 7 9 8 6 4 2

Typeset in Berling LT Std by Jojy Philip, New Delhi
Printed and bound in India by Replika Press Pvt. Ltd.

CONTENTS

INTRODUCTION

'Hope' is powerful. It enables a person to consider ways out of difficult, unpleasant or even near-impossible situations, mitigate stress and reduce the impact of disappointment and expectations in the present. Yet, hope can be often underestimated – its value lost in the privileged world in which some of us live. In this collection of essays, we bring together the conversations and experiences of those responsible for incarcerating individuals as well as the stories of those who have suffered incarceration.

It is often easy to forget those who are locked up behind bars. A prison is a complex space. The deepest dive that ordinary people can take into a prison often is through films or popular television series – whether of the Bollywood, Tollywood or Hollywood variety. Movies such as *Kaalia* (1981), *Umar Qaid* (1975), *Khuda Gawah* (1992), *Omkara* (2006) and *Bandit Queen* (1994), apart from scores of others, added grit, gore, glamour, while suffering from a lack of realism, barring the last two, to prison life. In Hollywood, *The Green Mile* (1999), *The Shawshank Redemption* (1994), *Papillon* (1973) and *Escape from Alcatraz* (1979) combined narratives of real or imagined events with strong research and scripts, good acting and large budgets. While there is vast international scholarship on prison conditions, serious research and books on the Indian prison system have been limited. There has been a trend in recent years to focus on famous subjects, such as people involved in sensational crimes or killings.

Generally, the approach of people on the subject of prisoners revolves around a feeling that 'they wouldn't be there if they hadn't done something'. Thus, conversations around prisoners and prison life are often restricted to incarcerated politicians or actors.

Rarely does someone think about prisons, or the criminal justice system itself, lest they find themselves or a family member or a friend in detention. This coupled with the fact that prisoners, denied the right to vote, are not a constituency – have largely meant that prisons remain neglected spaces that fall at the bottom of priority lists of the governments. To add to this dismal situation, the fact that prisons in India are state subjects, meaning that the state governments are empowered to frame laws and rules to regulate them, has resulted in stark differences between the way prisons are administered across the country – often, they are run as petty fiefdoms. Key choices about diet, amenities, recreation and release are made, usually arbitrarily, at the discretion of top officials, who have a free hand to make decisions about the lives of each prisoner in their custody. Even with statutory mandates for regular prison monitoring, oversight is mostly negligible.

Money, power, connections – caste, religion, gender – are considerations that gravely impact the treatment of persons during incarceration. This book aims to unravel some of these issues and enable a much more informed and nuanced understanding of prisons and the lives of prisoners in India.

Hope Behind Bars brings together a retired Supreme Court judge, former prison administrators, lawyers, journalists, academicians, researchers, a former prisoner and leaders of grassroots organizations. The effort is to shed light on the opaqueness of the system, making it not just more humane but also showing what can be achieved within the current ambits of the law, despite the infirmities of creaky and ineffective processes.

'Hope', in such conditions, is not just limited to prisoners. For those who engage with the prison system, hope often manifests in their activities and goals. A determination to improve conditions for prisoners, make an opaque system more transparent and accountable and ensure the practical realization of prisoners' rights is what pushes many of us to carry on. An intent to set in place practices which are sustainable, effective and productive encourages many who are part of the jail administrative system.

The collection is headlined with a powerful essay by former Supreme Court Justice Madan B. Lokur on the rights of vulnerable prisoners. Next is the gut-wrenching story of Wahid, who spent ten years in prison on a terrorism case before a court pronounced him innocent, as recounted by Sunetra Choudhury. It resonates because of the details he provides of custodial violence, torture – physical and mental – and police arbitrariness.

In chapter three, Vrinda Grover, the celebrated Supreme Court human rights lawyer, traces how she navigated the ups and downs, twists and turns of the Hashimpura killings case, which took thirty years to conclude: the case involved the Uttar Pradesh Provincial Armed Constabulary (PAC), which was charged with gunning down forty-two Muslims in the Hashimpura area of Muzaffarnagar, less than a hundred kilometres from New Delhi. The perils of prolonged judicial delays were underlined in this case – three of the accused died during this period.

Chapter four is an essay by Deepan Kumar Sarkar, a young Kolkata-based lawyer, who addresses questions of life and liberty, lawyers and prisoners. This is followed by a strong piece by Chaman Lal, a top police official who served in Punjab, Nagaland, Madhya Pradesh and the Border Security Force, before taking up a role as a special rapporteur and monitor in the National Human

Rights Commission (NHRC) to protect the rights of prisoners. S. Ramakrishnan, former Additional Director General of Police and Correctional Services, West Bengal and Director, Regional Institute of Correctional Administration, Kolkata, writes in chapter six about the challenges of establishing a prison training institute and the critical need to train prison officials.

Researchers from the Commonwealth Human Rights Initiative (CHRI) bring in their perspectives: Sabika Abbas and Sugandha Mathur write about what goes on in their minds during prison visits; their efforts to understand and to mitigate conditions. They come across inmates who, after crossing international borders to see film stars, have subsequently languished in prison for several years because of entering the country illegally.

Sangeeta Barooah Pisharoty provides a poignant description of life inside a detention centre in Assam in chapter eight and of the uncertainty that haunts lakhs who are not on the National Register of Citizens (NRC) in the state. Amrita Paul, also a researcher with CHRI, follows the story out of Assam in a study, which highlights the dilemma faced by refugees/asylum seekers confined in Indian prisons – the perils of freedom versus infinite detention. Focus is also brought to a lightly documented category of persons – the children of prisoners – in chapter ten by K. R. Raja, who highlights their secondary vulnerabilities and invisible suffering.

A prison is a world of its own, where residents live without the support systems that those on the outside take for granted. Prisoners hope and will each day to be their last in confinement. We believe that the stories in *Hope Behind Bars* provide insight into lives less ordinary.

Sanjoy Hazarika and Madhurima Dhanuka
11 April 2021

1

THE RIGHTS OF VULNERABLE PRISONERS

MADAN B. LOKUR

Rights of Prisoners

Prisoners are a vulnerable group whose human rights are consistently trampled upon by prison authorities and the State. Sunil Batra and Charles Sobhraj, both convicted of serious crimes, highlighted the plight of prisoners while they were serving their sentence in Tihar Jail. They pleaded before the Supreme Court that even prisoners have fundamental rights, though the exercise of those rights is limited due to the situation they are in. The Supreme Court intervened on their behalf and set off a chain of events that led to the recognition of the human rights of prisoners, including abolishing bar fetters and solitary confinement. Unfortunately, there is still a long way to go for more meaningful reforms, but the CHRI has restarted the process through extensive research and studies, thus proving itself instrumental in bringing about positive changes.

Two Principal Challenges

A few years ago, Justice Lahoti, a former Chief Justice of India, sent a letter to the then Chief Justice highlighting the extremely sorry state of prisoners' living conditions. The issues highlighted by Justice Lahoti included those of overcrowding and custodial deaths. After hearing all parties, the Supreme Court gave directions which led to some progress, but the problem of overcrowding persists. There are still so many prisons in the country with more than 150 per cent capacity and, in some cases, more than 200 per cent. In this context, it is essential to acknowledge that even the most hardened criminals have the right to live with dignity and, as pointed out by the Supreme Court, while some fundamental rights are restricted and some are not available to prisoners, they have the basic right to life of dignity. Overcrowding prohibits them from the exercise of this right.

Custodial deaths in prisons are by the dozen. There are several reasons for this, including natural causes, but a large number of deaths are due to suicides caused by depression, intimidation and browbeating by fellow prisoners, lack of adequate medical care and attention and other factors. It is in this context also that prison reforms are essential.

Rights of Under-trial Prisoners

It is tragic that the human rights of under-trial prisoners, that is, those who have not yet been convicted of an offence but are only accused or are suspects, are routinely trampled upon. Review committees for under-trial prisoners are said to be operational in every district of the country. They are tasked with scrutinizing the case of every under-trial prisoner so that wherever possible, they can be released. I have serious reservations about their efficacy and the effectiveness of their deliberations. Their casual approach to the task at hand makes prison reform that much more difficult.

Women Prisoners

Among the more vulnerable prisoners are women prisoners, many of whom perforce bring their children to prison to take care of them. These children have not committed any offence except perhaps the offence of being born to a woman now in custody, but they too have to suffer incarceration, at least for a few years, if not more. Do these women and children not have any human rights? Are we not expected to show some concern for them as well?

Access to Justice

Even though we have theoretical access to justice and a developing human rights jurisprudence, there is a need to address accessibility to justice. Are we providing justice-oriented procedures and support systems such as infrastructure and good quality representation? Times are changing and we need to change with the times; our jurisprudence must not be limited by the past. There is a dire need to look at some of the modern facilities that are available to us, such as advanced technology and improved infrastructure in the form of videoconferencing. These can make access to justice a reality for those behind prison bars.

Child-friendly and Witness-friendly Courts

Today there is considerable discussion on child-friendly courts so that juveniles in conflict with law and child victims, particularly victims of child sexual abuse, are kept away from a hostile court environment. Similarly, there are women and children who have survived sexual crimes and need to testify in courts. For them, vulnerable witness courts are necessary and, in fact, in some places, child-friendly courts double up as vulnerable witness courts. These are changes that may not directly impact the development of jurisprudence, but they have a long-term, indirect impact on justice delivery, which in turn will produce better quality justice, particularly for vulnerable persons.

Accessibility to justice also includes physical access. How many of our courts are disabled-friendly? How many of our courts can be easily accessed by illiterate or semi-literate litigants? While access to justice is certainly a human right, accessibility to justice is equally a human right that must be addressed, recognized and appreciated. Changes brought about in accessibility to justice will certainly bring in some degree of timeliness in disposing cases and expediting justice for the litigants, which are recognized human rights.

Legal Representation

We also need to look at the quality of representation available to litigants. Sometimes it is said that legal aid for the poor is poor legal aid. As the person once in charge of the Supreme Court Legal Services Committee, I am willing to confess that several changes need to be made to make access to justice a reality. The CHRI is assisting the Committee on some aspects of software development and, hopefully, things will improve in due course of time. Nevertheless, the concern remains one of providing effective access through effective representation.

The Way Forward

What is the way forward in the recognition and implementation of the human right to expeditious justice, not only for those accused of a crime but even generally? We need to seriously consider case management, a topic that has been discussed for more than a decade despite no productive results. We also need to discuss issues of judicial impact assessment through the introduction of new statutes. There was a time when the justice delivery system was virtually crippled by hundreds and thousands of cases related to cheque bounce. The wounds inflicted on justice delivery as a result of the Negotiable Instruments Act have not yet healed.

Stringent laws such as the Narcotic Drugs and Psychotropic Substances Act, 1985, have resulted in the loss of personal liberty of a large number of persons by denying bail, also complicating issues of human rights and justice delivery. There is, therefore, a clear need for introducing a judicial impact assessment whenever a law is tabled in the Parliament.

Judicial reforms must be sustained and procedures must be institutionalized, including process re-engineering, with the introduction of technology and computers in the justice delivery system needing serious consideration. Profound and systemic changes are required so that violations of human rights, particularly in cases of personal liberty, such as grant or denial of bail, the release of under trial prisoners and cases relating to the provision of social justice to vulnerable sections of society are addressed.

Our jurisprudence and constitutionalism can develop only if the pillars of democracy work towards a common goal and not towards damaging or destroying one another. The time has come for us to stand up and be counted.

2

WAHID AND THE DIFFERENT SHADES OF TORTURE[1]

SUNETRA CHOUDHURY

It was a day before Independence Day in 2006 when twenty-nine-year-old English teacher Wahid Sheikh learnt the nuances of torture in custody. His students at the Maulana Anjuman-i-Islam Abdul Sattar Shoaib School, a government-aided school in Mumbai, had no idea that their teacher was about to go on a long, long break – several years long, in fact.

On 11 July 2006 when 187 people were killed as seven explosions shattered the first-class general compartment of seven Mumbai local trains, Wahid may have been listening to the breaking news with his neighbour Munna at his Mumbra flat, but he wasn't surprised at getting a call from the police later in the evening. As usual, they asked him where he was and with whom.

'They took my name, address and job and how many family members I had. They were speaking nicely to us. They said ok, please give us details of where you can be reached and your school number (since I didn't have a mobile). They typed, they

[1] Excerpted from *Behind Bars: Prison Tales of India's Most Famous* by Sunetra Choudhury, New Delhi: Roli Books, 2017.

wrote it down too. The senior inspector who was talking said stay wherever but we will call you again perhaps.'

Wahid, a teacher there since 1999, went to the headmaster's room and found three police officers waiting for him. They wanted him to come along with them to the Crime Branch office and knowing the drill, he told a colleague to let his family know since 'those people would not release me soon'. He had barely sat in the car when they started beating and abusing him. At the office of the DCP Railways near Byculla (W) railway station, there was some more beating and abuse, after which he was put in the lockup. He was photographed, his fingerprints taken and then the wait started for the boss, Inspector Vijay Salaskar to arrive. The inspector, who was awarded the Ashoka Chakra after being killed in action during the Mumbai Terror attack of 2008, came at 9 p.m. and asked him about the train blasts. Wahid denied any involvement and after telling him not to leave the area, Salaskar finally let him go at 10 p.m.

After this twelve-hour long interrogation and beatings, Wahid went to school the next day and they all took part in the flag-hoisting. Only his headmaster knew about his ordeal. There was a bit of a reprieve for the next two days, but then again on 17 August three Anti-Terrorism Squad (ATS) officers knocked at the door of his one-room flat at 2 a.m. His wife, his two-year-old son and a newborn daughter were also at home. Wahid told his wife what he was told, that he had to go with them but he'd be back soon.

This time, they didn't wait for him to get into their Tata Sumo. The beatings started as soon as he walked outside the building. The questions were now more intimidating than before – they asked who was with him during the train blasts, and when he said he didn't know anything about them, they responded with sticks and kicks.

Wahid had told the court all this several times over but ten years later, what he still can't get over is that he was accused of being a terror plotter when he was actually going to the police station every single time he was summoned after 7/11.

Summing up the absurdity of the situation he says, 'Is it possible that a man after choreographing a bomb blast will keep appearing for questioning during its probe? That he will come for interrogation and then be released and then come back?

'The earlier torture was to just strip you, starve you one day and force feed you another, give religious *gaalis*, deny you sleep for 9–10 days – it was first and second degree. In third degree, they strip you, stretch your legs at 180 degrees and tear it, so your private parts start bleeding. Sometimes, they take something called Surya Prakash oil and inject it into your anus – which creates burning. They use the *chakki patta* to beat your hands and feet and then waterboard you (put you on a see-saw, head down and then put water, which gives you the feeling that you are drowning). The other forms are that they put you in a dark room for many days blindfolded so hard that your eyes feel like they are literally being corroded, and that even if you open your eyes in light, you aren't able to see anything.'

If you ask police officers about allegations of torture, they always point out that the system is now such that it is impossible to torture someone and get away with it. However, that's only half true. Yes, there are systems in place to check police excesses. Systems like mandatory medical tests for accused in police custody so that they can be physically examined for bruises, cuts, or fractures. But over and over again, in sworn testimony after sworn testimony, the accused point out that the way the police officers get away with this is that they have an understanding with medical examiners. In this case, all the tortured point out that the doctors wouldn't even examine them because they didn't want to act against the police. As Muzammil described it, during his examination: 'The police used to give some ointment to apply on the marks and the marks used to go away after 2–3 days and then again I used to be beaten. It is true that I was taken to the hospital every alternate day during police custody. I was taken to the doctor on the days prior and after the day on which advocate Shahid Azmi came to meet me. But I was not examined and only my thumb impression was taken.'

These horror stories of tormentor policemen who were all decorated officers came out during the trial when the accused realized that the worst had already happened to them. They were already languishing in jail and they had no deals to make. But, initially, they all kept quiet out of fear and threats and this was also used against them later when the judge asked why they'd kept quiet for so long.

It wasn't just these two officers who showed unease with their means, but also officer Khanvilkar. Wahid remembers how by the end of October 2006, he came and told him that he knew he was innocent, and that they had detained him illegally but he had to do what his bosses tell him. The same officers who had unleashed captive cruelty were now almost showing signs of remorse. 'He prayed with folded hands to forgive him and promised that he would do something to help me.'

Just a few days later, on 3 November, an anonymous letter written by an ATS officer emerged. The letter addressed to the president, to the home minister and others talked about the illegal detention of the accused, their innocence and the pressure that the officers faced in booking them for the entire case. The letter stated that ATS officers were ashamed that innocents were being framed, but the then home minister R. R. Patil reacted to this by saying no heed should be paid to all this.

It took the Malegaon men ten years to clear their name, and it took Wahid almost the same time. The twelve others have been sentenced to death. But for his freedom, Wahid had to credit his courage to not confess and his brother-in-law, Quraishi.

All the other accused retracted their confessions in court but the judge did not believe them.

In 2015, the court finally told the English teacher from Mumbra: 'Prosecution has not been able to prove any independent circumstance to show that A8 (Wahid) harboured.'

Wahid was finally free to go home to his wife and children; his daughter he'd barely known since she was just a newborn and his son only two years old when he was picked up. His wife, he says, never stepped out of home before but now was working as a schoolteacher because someone needed to pay for them. 'My daughter was never breastfed because of this.' Wahid's father died just a year after he went to jail, and so did his mother-in-law. His mother was in depression but now seems to be doing better. In January 2017, Wahid and his wife had another baby boy.

The other bright spark for Wahid is that his community has welcomed him back. Wahid went back to teaching in his school, although they are yet to give him his salary (the government says wait and watch in case an appeal is filed). His old students have been regular visitors, coming to check up on their teacher. 'The colleagues, students and neighbours, they all are fine with me, happy and welcoming. Only the Government of Maharashtra feels I am a terrorist, nobody else feels that.' In 2016, Wahid started a campaign called 'The Innocence Network'. It had only one objective – to get acquittals for the twelve who were still on death row and to campaign against the use of [the Unlawful Activities (Prevention) Act, 1967 (UAPA)] to harass citizens.

3

FROM IMPUNITY TO ACCOUNTABILITY

UNLOCKING THE LABYRINTH OF THE HASHIMPURA KILLINGS (1987–2018)[2]

VRINDA GROVER

Thirty-four years ago, in May 1987, communal violence gripped Meerut district, in Uttar Pradesh (U.P.), around 90 kilometres away from Delhi. The trigger for this was the decision of the Union government headed by Prime Minister Rajiv Gandhi, in 1986, to open the locks of the Babri Masjid in order to allow Hindu worshippers to enter, which led to an outbreak of rioting. At the time, a Congress government led by Chief Minister Veer Bahadur Singh was in place in the state of UP.

On a hot summer afternoon of 22 May 1987, during the month of Ramzan, soon after the 'Alvida ki namaaz' was offered, a joint search-and-arrest operation was launched by the UP state police, the Provincial Armed Constabulary (PAC) and the Indian Army in Mohalla Hashimpura, a locality adjacent to Meerut town. Hashimpura housed predominantly Muslim residents, including migrants from Bihar, most of whom worked in home-based power loom units.

---

[2] This article has been developed from the CHRI's Annual Lecture in 2019 delivered by the author.

As Prosecution Witness (PW-4) Mujib-ur-Rehman stated in Court:

> I am a permanent resident of Distt. Darbhanga in Bihar. I started working on the power loom of Abdul Mazid *Incholia Wale* in Mohalla Hashimpura four years prior to the year 1987.

Perceiving the Muslim populace as the source of trouble, all the men of Hashimpura were rounded up and marched out of their homes as part of a strategy ostensibly for maintaining law and order by the law enforcement forces. A total of 644 able-bodied Muslim men were placed under arrest, loaded into PAC and army trucks and driven away to different police stations and jails.

Around forty to forty-five of the arrested Muslim men were loaded into a PAC vehicle, a yellow truck bearing the number URU-1493. The PAC platoon abducted them and drove them first to the Gang Nehar canal in Muradnagar and then to the neighbouring Hindon canal. At both the sites, the PAC personnel stopped the truck and used their official .303 rifles to shoot the captive men, dragging some of them down from the truck and shooting indiscriminately at those inside. The corpses were then thrown into the water.

Five young men survived this shootout and emerged from the bloodied water. They became the witnesses and chroniclers of the horrors of that night, who lived to tell their tale.

Timeline (1987–2018)

Two FIRs were registered. Within forty-eight hours, both the investigations were transferred to the Crime Branch–Criminal Investigation Department (CB-CID), Lucknow. For nine long years, the CB-CID investigated the killings. In 1996, a chargesheet against nineteen PAC personnel was filed before the court in Ghaziabad, UP. The accused PAC men brazenly refused to comply with the summons and did not appear before the court for six years.

In 2002, in response to a petition filed by the families of the victims, the trial was transferred to Delhi by the Supreme Court of India. Almost twenty years after the killings, in 2006, a Delhi Sessions Court finally began the examination of prosecution witnesses. In March 2015, almost two decades after the chargesheet was filed, the court acquitted all nineteen of the accused PAC personnel, three of whom had died during the course of the trial.

Appeals against the acquittal were filed in the Delhi High Court on behalf of the survivors and the victim families and also by the State of Uttar Pradesh. The National Human Rights Commission (NHRC) also approached the High Court and was impleaded in the case.

On 31 October 2018, thirty-one years after the macabre crime, the Delhi High Court judgment overturned the acquittal, convicted the sixteen surviving accused PAC men and sentenced them to life imprisonment for murder, criminal conspiracy, attempt to murder and destruction of evidence.

The convicted PAC men are now incarcerated in Tihar Jail, Delhi. They have filed appeals challenging their conviction that are pending before the Supreme Court.

The Trial and its Travails

The case, titled *State vs Surendra Pal Singh and Others* in the court docket, meandered on for almost thirty-two years in the labyrinth of the courts. All through these years, the victim community stood steadfast at the forefront of the struggle.

During the early years of the court battle, the victims formed the 'Hashimpura Legal Advisory Committee' (HLAC) with two highly respected elders as the convenors. Mohammed Yamin or Yamin Saab, as he was popularly called, who doggedly pursued the case, was always seen carrying a bag stuffed with legal documents. Yamin Saab, the motivating force behind the legal efforts, undoubtedly knew the case papers better than anyone else. Tragically, he did not live long enough to witness that his tireless efforts led to the men in uniform being held accountable. The co-convenor of the HLAC, Professor Harpal Singh, taught political science at Meerut University. Professor Singh's only son, a medical doctor, was murdered in the riots of May 1987, leaving behind a wife and two children. A member of the Communist Party of India (CPI) and an avowed secularist, Singh firmly believed that the killing of his son and others was not a justification for the custodial killing of Muslims of Hashimpura. Stoically carrying the burden of his irreparable loss, he gave unstinting support to this struggle for justice.

The imperative of fair trial demanded that the case be transferred to Delhi. But it also meant that the witnesses and the victim community had to find the time and resources to travel to Delhi repeatedly to attend multiple court hearings at the Tis Hazari court. For these fruit vendors, daily wage earners, labourers and widows, each trip meant losing a day's wages. Yet, despite their trauma, fear, poverty and exhaustion, they pursued the trial for thirty-one long years.

It used to take about three hours to travel from Hashimpura to Delhi. I recall one of the early hearings when the families of the victims came to the Tis Hazari court in Delhi. Most of them were widowed women – wives and mothers of the men who had been killed. Seeing this motley group of a dozen odd burkha-clad women accompanied by Muslim men wearing skull caps inside the court room, a lawyer said to the judge, 'I think this crowd should be searched.' Thus 'attending court while Muslim', even as victims, was enough to provoke alarm and anxiety. Fortunately, the judge did not perceive women in burqas and men in skullcaps as a security threat.

In this arduous and long legal struggle, the victims' families were represented in court by Sr Advocate Rebecca M. John and me. A small yet committed team of young lawyers – Vishal Gosain, Harsh Bora and Ratna Appnender – followed the trial tenaciously, with advocates Bhavook Chauhan, Soutik Banerjee and Megha Bahl joining the legal team at the appellate stage. Friends and colleagues advised me that it was pointless to fight this case, which they dubbed 'a lost cause'. Despite their sage advice, our commitment to the victim families and our admiration for their courage and tenacity gave us the strength we needed to pursue the case.

As the trial crawled on, the victims were alarmed at the indifference and apathy of the prosecution, and as the Hashimpura massacre clocked twenty years, they demanded that the state appoint a Special Public Prosecutor, following which Sr Advocate Satish Tamta was appointed to conduct the trial.

Evidence

When a case is tried before a criminal court, it stands or falls on the evidence presented by the prosecution which, as the law mandates, must establish the guilt beyond reasonable doubt.

Was the Hashimpura massacre of over forty Muslim men a whodunnit? A macabre crime that left bloodstains but no trail? The primary evidence relied upon by the prosecution were the five young men who had fortuitously survived to recount the horror. The shooting left them scarred and wounded, with two of them permanently disabled by bullet injuries. These five men came forward and testified as star witnesses for the prosecution before the Delhi Trial Court.

Eyewitness Accounts

The five survivors were young men, aged between eighteen and twenty-one years at the time of the crime. Twenty years later, they stepped into the witness box to recount and relive the chilling details of the crime.

The first Prosecuting Witness, Zulfiqar Nasir, (PW 1) stated:

> On 22.5.1987, it was Zumma (Friday), I was reciting Namaz in the evening at about 6 p.m. on the roof of my house when few military persons came to my house. The said military persons took myself, my father, my two uncles (chachas) and my grandfather outside our house in the street on the road. The said military persons made us sit on the said road where already about 400–500 persons were sitting. Persons of our mohalla thus collected were sitting on both the sides of the road … I saw a big force of military and PAC deployed there. Seven or eight trucks belonging to military and PAC were also parked there. PAC persons divided the mohalla people into two groups. One group comprised elderly people and children whereas the second group was of young persons. They then ordered the group of young persons to sit in their trucks. PAC as well as the army people both took away the trucks after loading young persons from that place. My both chachas and my father were in the group of young persons who were taken away by PAC and military. I do not know as to where they were taken away. To the group of elderly people and the children left at the spot, PAC officials gave directions to maintain peace and go to their respective houses. Before they could leave for their houses, PAC officials segregated the able-bodied elderly persons and boys of my age. This way about 40–45 people were scrutinized and made to sit in the only truck left at the spot on which 'PAC' was written. I was in the said group of 40–45 people in the said truck. It was about 8 p.m. The said truck was yellow in colour and it bore the

> writing in white paint 'PAC'. PAC officials, after making us sit in the truck, gave us directions to keep our heads downwards and not to raise our head. There were 18–20 officials of PAC in the truck at that time. The PAC officials had surrounded us in the truck in such a manner that we were not visible to anyone outside.[1]

Mohammed Naeem (PW 2) too described the cold-blooded killings by the PAC men:

> ...PAC officials were carrying official rifles with them. They were also wearing black iron helmets on their heads. Some of the rifles were carrying Sangeen on their tops ... They all were in Peeli uniform. The truck reached Delhi road via P. L. Sharma road ... All of us were asked not to raise our heads while sitting in the truck. In case anybody tried to raise his head, he was hit. The truck then reached Murad Nagar, Gang Nehar and came to a halt at a place which was about 2 km away from Delhi road. The lights of the truck were switched off. It might have been 9:30 or 9:45 p.m. at that time. PAC jawans sitting in the cabin of the truck came down and surrounded the back of the truck in the form of a circle. First of all, they brought Yasin down from the truck and shot three bullets in his body. I heard the sound of said three bullet shots. After catching hold of his legs and arms, Mr Yasin was thrown into the *nehar*. They then brought down another boy from the truck who was also thrown in the nehar after being shot ... Similar treatment was given to another boy thereafter ... All of us sitting in the truck then stood up and shouted, '*bachao, bachao*' (Save us). At this the PAC jawans started firing inside the truck itself. The PAC jawans standing outside the truck started giving butt blows to the persons inside the truck. I was hit with the butt of the rifle on my stomach with the result that I fell to the floor of the truck. Three or four boys thereafter fell

[1] An extract translated from the evidence recorded in Hindi by the Trial Court.

> on me while I was lying in there. One of the said boys was Qamruddin, who had received a bullet injury. Qamruddin was alive at that time.[2]

Naeem escaped death because he lay still in the truck, covered with the blood of others. Assuming him to be dead, the PAC men threw his blood-soaked body into the canal. Later, he emerged from the water, without any bullet injury.

To this day, Mohammad Usman (PW 3), carries the scars of the PAC shooting; a scar marks the spot where a bullet fired into his stomach exited from his back. Another bullet left a scar etched on his thigh. These injuries have disabled him, rendering him incapable of working on the power loom. Today, he ekes out a living by selling fruits from a handcart.

Usman saw at least fifteen men being shot by the PAC, before being wounded himself. He told the court:

> We shouted 'bachao, bachao'. Upon this, the PAC jawans standing outside the truck and inside the truck started firing at all of us. They then started throwing the dead persons in the water and also fired again at anyone found alive. After killing about fifteen persons, came my turn. I tried to run away but two PAC jawans caught hold of me by my arm. I begged for mercy saying that my children would be rendered orphans. They did not take pity on me. In the meantime, a PAC jawan intervened and said, 'kill him right now'. At this, I attempted to snatch the rifle after freeing my arm from the hands of the PAC jawan. Immediately, a bullet was fired into my belly and the bullet came out from my back, the PAC jawans fired another shot which struck at my right leg and the bullet made its exit from the back side of my right thigh; thereafter, I was thrown in the water while I was writhing in pain.[3]

---

[2] An extract translated from the evidence recorded in Hindi at the Trial Court.

[3] An extract translated from the evidence recorded in Hindi at the Trial Court.

The PAC men stopped firing only when they saw the headlights of an approaching milk van. The truck then sped away towards the Hindon canal where the armed men unleashed another spree of firing on the remaining captives in the truck.

Babudeen (PW 11), on whose statement the second FIR in the case was lodged, described his ordeal:

> We raised hue and cry, the jawans of PAC kept firing, while we were held inside the truck. I sustained a bullet injury on the left side of my back. We were all thrown into the two different canals because some remained alive, they came out. The police of two different areas arrived at the sites of the killings. They heard bullet shots ... and learnt that there was something amiss. Then, they took the victims to the hospital.

Two FIRs were registered at the sites of the killings, one in P. S. Muradnagar and the other in P. S. Link Road.

Over forty Muslim men were shot, killed and dumped in the water by the PAC. Qamruddin, a young man married for just a month, died on the way to the hospital. One body was recovered from Kalyan Puri, in East Delhi, from where the Hindon canal joins the Yamuna River. The exact number of victims was never known as the bodies drowned and were not recovered.

Postmortems carried out on the corpses confirmed that all the dead men were circumcised, an unambiguous marker of their Muslim identity. Having targeted the men of Hashimpura for being Muslims, the state went ahead to obliterate every trace of the victims' Muslim identity. The bodies were not handed over to the families after the postmortem. Instead, the police unceremoniously cremated them, ensuring no evidence remained for exhumation in the future. Dignity was denied to the victims in life and death.

Another piece of unambiguous evidence presented before the court were the photographs clandestinely taken by eminent photographer Praveen Jain, who was working at the *Sunday Mail* at the time. Those photos depicted Muslim men being marched out of their homes in Mohalla Hashimpura, their arms raised in the air, with the police and other uniformed men pointing guns at them. The photographs allowed victim families to identify the men whom they had seen for the last time that fateful afternoon and who had disappeared without a trace. The photographs proved that the victims had been taken into custody. These black-and-white photographs later became iconic images of the Hashimpura killings.

Prior to the advent of digital photography, a picture had evidentiary value in the eyes of the law only if the negative was also exhibited. Jain had handed over his photographs to the CB-CID but kept the negatives safely in his own possession. Thus, only the photographs were annexed in the chargesheet before the court.

In 2010, when the case finally came up for trial more than twenty years later, this proved to be a blessing; we tracked down Praveen Jain who was then at the *Indian Express*. He scoured through his personal archive and dug out the negatives, which were then placed as evidence in the court. If he had not held back the original negatives, perhaps these too may have been suppressed or lost like other documentary evidence, in the control of the state.

Erasure of Evidence

All through the long and tortuous course of the Hashimpura case, it was a challenge to fill the gaps created by the loss, erasure, suppression and destruction of material evidence. The prosecution witnesses in their deposition in court affirmed that on the night of the incident, the district magistrate and SP of Ghaziabad rushed to the motor transport section of the PAC Headquarters in Ghaziabad, where the yellow PAC truck number URU-1493, which had carried the men to their deaths, was parked. Witnesses confirmed that around the midnight of 22 May 1987, the truck was washed, leaving puddles of bloodstained water. A bullet hole could be seen in the metal body of the truck. Yet, the truck was not seized, and no forensic examination was conducted till a year later.

Similarly, the .303 rifles and the murder weapons were never sent for forensic examination to the FSL laboratory. Even before the trial commenced, the rifles which formed case property in a mass murder, were casually returned to the PAC for use, thus rupturing the chain of forensic evidence.

Acquittal by the Trial Court

The five eyewitnesses and survivors of the massacre, deposing as prosecution witnesses, testified against the PAC accused with courage and honesty. They described the gruesome killings in graphic detail and stated clearly that policemen wearing a *khaki peeli* or brownish-yellow-coloured uniform abducted them in a yellow PAC truck and shot them using their rifles with bayonets. However, they admitted that they could neither name nor identify the PAC men who sprayed bullets into the truck and threw the corpses into the water.

Pronouncing its judgment in March 2015, the Delhi Sessions Court acknowledged: 'The present case relates to a horrific incident of targeted abduction and killing of around 42 persons by the officers of the PAC, a reserve police force of the State of UP on the night of 22.5.1987.' The court acquitted all the PAC accused, holding: 'From the material available on record, the identity of the actual culprit has not been established and the material is not sufficient to connect the accused persons facing trial with the alleged offence.'

The Sessions Court concluded that the prosecution had failed to establish and prove the culprits' identity beyond reasonable doubt. The missing link was the material evidence required to connect the specific nineteen PAC accused personnel with the commission of the crime; however, the killings by PAC personnel itself stood proved.

While acquitting the accused, the Trial Court found the incident proved and awarded compensation to the five survivors and families of four arbitrarily chosen victims. The compensation order by the Trial Court is prima facie erroneous in that it awards monetary compensation only to four of the victim families. The order was challenged by the victims in the Delhi High Court, which directed the state of UP to pay compensation to the survivors and the families of the deceased in accordance with the provisions of Section 357A CrPC and the relevant compensation scheme adopted by the state. Section 357A mandates that every state and central government shall compensate the victim or his dependents who have suffered loss or injury from the crime and require rehabilitation. It is revealing that the state did not even care to appeal against this flawed order. It was the counsel for the victims, Sr Advocate Rebecca M. John, who appealed against this order and secured compensation for all the injured survivors and the victim families from the Delhi High Court. Finally, each of the victim families received a total amount of ₹10 lakhs, while the survivors received compensation of ₹5 lakhs each.

The Missing Link

In India, paperwork is the hallmark of official activity. The functioning of the police too involves detailed documentation and creates a paper trail that inscribes their movements and activities. All police personnel are statutorily required to record an entry, in the daily diary or general diary register, whenever they leave for duty and again when they return to the police station. No rifle, arms or ammunition can be taken out of the police station without their description, details and numbers being recorded in the relevant register. A corresponding entry is made when the weapons are returned to the police station. Similarly, every police vehicle is required to make an entry in the vehicle logbook before each journey, and record the route, fuel consumption, purpose, destination and the name of the driver.

There is no mystery about the location of these records, and the responsibility and accountability for their safekeeping – all these records are in the exclusive custody and control of the PAC and/or the state of UP. Given that the CB-CID was engaged in this investigation for nine years, it is reasonable to assume that they conducted a rigorous and thorough investigation and that all relevant documents collected were filed with the chargesheet in court. However, during the protracted trial, it emerged that the original registers – the evidence linking the accused to the crime – were missing from the judicial record.

Victims' Appeal Against the Acquittals

The Trial Court acquittal led to an outcry and revived the public debate on impunity for mass crimes committed by men in uniform. The petitioners, steadfast in their quest for justice, decided to appeal against the acquittal in the Delhi High Court.

The victims' appeal was argued before the court by Sr Advocate Rebecca John, who worked pro bono and represented the petitioners' case with her inimitable professional rigour and passion.

The main challenge in the appeal was to establish beyond doubt the provenance of the truck in which the victims were abducted, and the identities of the PAC men who committed the killings.

Intervention of the NHRC

Over the years, questions have been raised about the reluctance of the NHRC to exercise its statutory powers, preferring instead to pose as 'a toothless tiger'.[4] Although the NHRC holds the statutory power to challenge grave injustice, it has intervened legally in very few instances. The Gujarat pogrom against Muslims in 2002 was one such occasion when the NHRC filed a petition before the Supreme Court. The Hashimpura case is another. Recognizing the acquittals as a grave miscarriage of justice, the NHRC impleaded itself in the appeal proceedings, and I represented the NHRC before the Delhi High Court.

The law permits additional evidence to be produced even at the appellate stage in some circumstances. On behalf of the NHRC, I filed an application under Section 391 of the Code of Criminal Procedure, pointing out the suppression and destruction of material evidence and asked that the state of UP and the PAC be directed to produce the original record of documents in their control and custody. These documents included general diary registers, duty registers, attendance registers, logbooks and other materials where the names, duty rosters, postings and other relevant details of the men of the 41st Battalion of C Company, who were on riot control duty under Commandant Surender Pal Singh on 22 May 1987 at Hashimpura, were scribed.

These documents were the missing link in the case: the material evidence that connected the accused to the crime, the missing link in the chain of circumstantial evidence.

The document recording the entry and exit of personnel of 'C' Company, 41st Battalion, PAC, was finally unearthed from the state archives after much persuasion. After multiple

---

[4] Apoorva Mandhani, 'NHRC Has Been Reduced To A Toothless Tiger: Supreme Court [Read Judgment]', Livelaw.in, 14 July 2017. Available: https://www.livelaw.in/nhrc-reduced-toothless-tiger-supreme-court-read-judgment/.

obfuscations, when it was clear that the High Court would not relent, the state of UP provided a photocopy of the relevant portion of the general diary. The state claimed that the photocopy was already on record as a part of the chargesheet.

The photocopy of a document has no evidentiary value in the eyes of the law. To constitute admissible evidence, the original document has to be produced and proved in court. In another desperate attempt to mislead the court, the state claimed that certain documents had been 'weeded out'. The response from the court was firm – action for destruction of evidence would be taken against the officer who ordered the 'weeding out'. The state was asked to submit an affidavit and declare the name of the officer who allowed weeding out of documents while the trial was ongoing.

Having run out of options, the PAC was forced to admit that the original general diary register was, and always had been, in their possession. In 2017, the original document was produced for the first time before the Delhi High Court. The CB-CID was compelled to place this vital document on record as evidence, which it was either unable or unwilling to do for thirty years.

The *ravangi* or departure entry in the general diary (GD) register, proved to be the proverbial final nail in the coffin, as it records the date and time of entry and exit of the PAC platoon; enumerates the names of all the PAC personnel dispatched for duty; notes the registration number of the PAC vehicle assigned to the platoon as truck URU-1493; and details the number of arms and ammunitions assigned to the PAC platoon. It notes that the accused PAC men left for 'riot duty' to Meerut district on 22 May 1987.

In view of the resurrection of the original document, the Delhi High Court directed the Trial Court to record the additional evidence. Of the four investigating officers who investigated this case over nine years, only one of them, now in his eighties, was fortunately still alive.

Ranbir Singh Bishnoi, the investigating officer, appeared as PW 72 and identified and authenticated the general diary before the Trial Court, placing this clinching evidence on record. In his cross-examination PW 72 Ranbir Singh Bishnoi stated:

> According to GD No. 6 (part of Ex. PW-72/A), on 22.05.1987 at 7:50 a.m. police force was sent to Out Post Pilokhadi, PS Lisadi Gate, Meerut, UP. According to GD No. 6, PC Surender Pal Singh along with his section having H Ct. Niranjan Lal, Naik Rambir Singh, Ct. Om Prakash, Ct. Shami Ullah, Ct. Jai Pal, Ct. Mahesh Prasad, H Ct. Suresh Chand Sharma, H Ct. Kamal Singh, Ct. Ram Dhyan, Ct. Sarwan Kumar, Ct. Leela Dhar, Ct. Hambir Singh, H Ct. Kush Kumar, Ct. Kunwar Pal, Ct. Budha Singh and Ct. Basant Ballabh went to Out Post Pilokhadi.
>
> As per the said GD, at that time, they had 17 rifles, 850 rounds, one revolver with 30 rounds, and they had gone there in the truck bearing registration no. URU 1493 and the name of the driver of the said truck was Ct. Mohkam Singh.

The same GD register at Entry number 15 notes the return of this platoon of the PAC accused men.

For three decades, this register kept the names of the accused men secret, burying them in the crevices of the state legal apparatus. The determined struggle of the victims and their lawyers helped finally exhume the truth and conclusively establish the identity of the perpetrators.

This clinching documentary evidence enabled the court to ascertain the identity of the perpetrators. The High Court held that the involvement of the accused in the crime had been more than adequately established through contemporaneous evidence in the form of GD registers, and none of the accused had actually denied their presence in Meerut or denied using this truck. The High Court, therefore, held that this was a case of criminal conspiracy.

Custodial Killing

The High Court judgment is pathbreaking on many counts, not least because it significantly advances our jurisprudence on mass crimes by recognizing the massacre as custodial crimes. Thus far, custodial deaths were defined as deaths occurring within the physical confines of a police lock-up or prison. The High Court judgment recognized the Hashimpura massacre as an incidence of deemed custody, where liberty had been restrained by State actors:

> Although the victims were not taken to an enclosed place by the PAC, they were unlawfully detained. Kept in the PAC truck and taken to two places and were asked to keep their heads down and not allowed to move. This leads this court to conclude that they were kept in unlawful custody by the accused purporting to discharge the official function when the fact is they were clearly acting illegally.

This position also aligns with the recommendations of both the Law Commission of India and the Supreme Court – for purposes of custodial crimes, 'custody' must be recognized as extending beyond the prison or lock-up to the entire sphere of control and authority of the men in uniform. The Hashimpura case sets an important precedent in the docket of accountability for custodial killings.

Mala fide Investigation and State Complicity

The High Court judgment enumerates a long list of 'lapses' in the investigation. In my view, these are not 'lapses' or inadvertent errors made by the investigating agency but rather indicators of State complicity and mala fide investigation in a case of custodial killings.

Targeted Killings

The Delhi High Court judgment points out that this massacre was not a random incident of cops 'going berserk' or becoming 'trigger-happy', but a case of targeted killing of Muslim men. The court further located the targeted killing within the larger framework of institutional bias. In the Trial Court, the defence had argued that no motive had been attributed to the PAC personnel for the mass murders. The Delhi High Court observed:

> A disturbing aspect of the present case is a targeted killing of persons belonging to one minority community. It was submitted on behalf of the accused that the prosecution in the present case has not proved a motive of the crime and since the 42 persons allegedly abducted were total strangers, the accused had no grudge or animosity against them and much less the members of a disciplined force than the accused would commit such a gruesome crime.
>
> What the above submission overlooks is the fact that all the victims belonged to a minority community. This was a case of a targeted killing revealing an institutional bias within the law enforcement agents in this case.

The High Court verdict quotes a study of the Centre for Developing Societies and Common Cause based on data from twenty-four states of India, showing there is an institutional bias in the police force against the Muslim community. This provides compelling reason to revisit the juridical category of motive in cases of State violence.

Institutional racism, or institutional bias as a jurisprudential category, was first articulated by Lord MacPherson in his report enquiring into the killing of Stephen Lawrence, a young black man in the United Kingdom. The Delhi High Court judgment in the Hashimpura massacre case similarly urges that institutional biases embedded in our State institutions and machinery, directed against Muslims, Christians, Dalits, Adivasis, women, transgenders, the poor and other 'less equal' groups in our society, are acknowledged and addressed.

Right to Know the Truth

The High Court judgment underscores the 'Right to know the Truth', a legal principle recognized under international law, especially in cases of enforced disappearances. This principle was also articulated by Justice Lokur in the Supreme Court judgment of the Manipur extrajudicial killings case (*Extra Judicial Execution Victim Families Association [EEVFAM] vs Union of India*). The Delhi High Court judgment in the Hashimpura case recognizes the right to know the truth as integral to the victim's right to justice. The judgement urges the state to take necessary steps to put a working mechanism in place to secure and protect this right.

Gaps in Law

The Hashimpura case forces us to reconfigure the paradigm within which police accountability is located. An aspect of speculation was whether this killing spree by the PAC was triggered by the order of Surendra Pal Singh, the commandant of PAC 41C battalion, or whether the signal for the massacre came from a superior officer or a political master, whose culpability had not yet been brought to light.

Under international criminal law, the doctrine of command responsibility or superior responsibility enables the proverbial long arm of the law to assign criminal liability and bring to book a superior officer or commander, within whose knowledge, effective control and authority the crimes took place and who failed to take measures to prevent and punish the perpetrators. The absence of this doctrine in India's legal lexicon has emboldened and enabled the actual masterminds in many horrific crimes to escape accountability.

Another significant issue for legislative reform that emerges from the Hashimpura case is the responsibility for preservation of evidence. Research and documentation carried out by citizens' groups confirms the inclination of the State to shield its offending functionaries. While procedural safeguards exist in the form of NHRC Guidelines in cases of extrajudicial killings, fake encounters and custodial deaths, these have been largely ignored with impunity. There is an urgent need to develop a more robust system to track the insidious tentacles of State complicity and ensure accountability and punishment not only for the planners and perpetrators of the crime but also for those responsible for destruction of evidence and mala fide investigation.

Very often, judicial verdicts, even as they censure and castigate the police and investigators, stop short of directing civil and criminal action against them. Barring a few noteworthy exceptions like the judgment of the Bombay High Court in the Bilkis Bano case and the EEVAFM judgment of the Supreme Court, there appears to be some hesitation in holding the police accountable for mala fide and illegal investigation, including custodial torture.

The morale of the men in uniform is usually cited as a good reason for the court to turn a blind eye to their excesses. This argument begs the question of how this impunity for criminals in uniform impinges on the morale of citizens in our constitutional democracy, who place their faith in the criminal legal system and their inalienable right to justice.

Recourse to Right to Information Law

In the long journey of the Hashimpura case, the Right to Information (RTI) law was used strategically at several points, both to access information and to highlight the institutional apathy towards the plight of the victims of what is arguably the bloodiest incident of custodial communal killings in independent India.

To mark the twentieth year of their ongoing struggle for justice, in 2007, the victim families travelled to Lucknow, seeking answers. At the time, the 2005 RTI statute was mainly used to call out corruption and seek answers from government agencies and functionaries. For the first time since its adoption, the RTI Act was used to challenge the impunity of the State and seek accountability from the men in uniform.

On the morning of 22 May 2007, family members of the Hashimpura victims, two of the survivors, Mohd. Yamin of the Legal Advisory Committee and I, accompanied by a delegation of public-spirited citizens of Lucknow, reached the office of the Director General of Police (DGP) of the city to file RTI applications. In the evening, the victims addressed a crowded press conference in Lucknow, where they spoke about their struggle, voiced their anguish and expressed outrage at the indifference of the State to their plight, as indicated by the lethargy in pursuing the criminal case. Their firm resolve to continue the struggle was reflected in the words on their banner, '*Intezaar Hai, Himmat Chahiye, Himmat hai, Insaaf Chahiye*' (we are waiting, we need courage; we have courage, we want justice).

The families of each of the forty-two victims and the five survivors asked the State for the following information, about each of the nineteen PAC accused men, through their 613 RTI applications.

- Were the nineteen accused PAC men suspended from service? Provide a copy of the order of suspension and revocation of suspension.
- Was any departmental inquiry initiated against them?
- Was any disciplinary action taken against them?

- Or were they rewarded with promotions in rank and emoluments?
- Copies of the Annual Confidential Report (ACR) of each of the nineteen PAC accused men from 1987–2006.

As counsel for the victims, I filed two RTI applications with the U.P. Home Department, seeking information regarding the protracted investigation.

- Copy of the Inquiry Report submitted by the CB-CID into the Hashimpura killings of Muslims by the PAC;
- How many persons were indicted by the CB-CID Report in the PAC Killings?
- Complete list of the names and ranks of all PAC persons and any others indicted in the CB-CID report;
- Why did the State sanction criminal prosecution only against nineteen PAC men and not all those indicted in the CB-CID Report?
- When was the inquiry into the Hashimpura killings by the PAC handed over to the CB-CID? Why did it take the CB-CID six to seven years to complete the inquiry? What were the reasons for the delay?
- The CB-CID submitted the Report to the U.P. State Government in February 1994; why was the chargesheet filed only in May 1996? What were the reasons for the delay of over two years? Who was responsible for this delay?

Replies to the 613 RTIs were received within the statutory period of thirty days. The answers are a shameful exposé of the complicity of the State in the massacre through acts of omission and commission.

The RTI replies were an official admission that no disciplinary enquiry or departmental proceedings were ever initiated against the nineteen PAC accused. Although charged and facing trial for committing multiple murders while on duty, none of the accused was dismissed from service. All the accused men were suspended for brief periods, varying from a year to a maximum of two years. The case of the platoon commandant accused Surendra Pal Singh is illustrative. He was suspended from the PAC for three months (from 20 September 1995 to 3 December 1996). On 2 December 1996, he filed an application seeking restoration to service, citing 'financial difficulties'. His suspension order was revoked on the very next day, by an order that looks like a cyclostyled copy of orders passed for the co-accused. His suspension was promptly revoked by the PAC stating that as it was facing a shortage of men, he should be brought back on duty.

Throughout the long trial, the PAC accused remained in service and were posted as armed policemen across UP, including on election duty. The suspension and revocation record conclusively demonstrated that the police leadership did not consider the accused PAC men unfit to bear arms despite being charged and prosecuted for the mass murder of innocent men in their custody, for no reason other than their religious identity.

The performance reports of the accused for the period 1987–2006, disclosed in reply to the 613 RTIs, provide a rare window into the internal workings of the police establishment. In the PAC documents, all traces of the massacre have been erased. The performance reports do not contain even a whisper about the killings, the investigation, prosecution and trial, even in the crucial years of 1996 when the chargesheet was filed, and 2006, when the charges of murder were framed and the eyewitness survivors gave evidence in court. It was as if the PAC was completely unaware of the ongoing criminal trial. The accused men were commended for their achievements in sports, praised for their discipline and integrity and awarded high grades of 'good' and 'very good' in the ACR.

स्वस्थ व स्मार्ट जवान है। वाहिनी फुटबॉल टीम का सदस्य है। वर्ष में दो नगद पुरस्कार व दो G. E. पाया है।

कार्य व आचरण अच्छा है। सत्यनिष्ठा प्रमाणित है।

श्रेणी – अच्छा 28/2/88

सीधा व अनुशाषित जवान है। काम में रूचि लेता है। वाहिनी स्तर का फुटबॉल खिलाडी है। वर्ष में दो G. E. व एक Reward पाया है।

कार्य व आचरण अच्छा है। सत्यनिष्ठा प्रमाणित है।

श्रेणी – अच्छा 23/1/89

The efficacy of internal mechanisms of accountability within the police machinery has been an important issue of debate in the police reform campaign. This case raises many disturbing questions. What is the status accorded to human rights within the police system, beyond lip service and platitudes, by higher-ups at academic conferences or ceremonial occasions? Are the bonds of 'brotherhood of Khaki' so strong that law cannot pierce through to secure accountability?

Conclusion

In 2006, the Supreme Court in the Prakash Singh judgment issued a slew of directions to insulate the police from extraneous influences, particularly the executive, by giving senior police officers some degree of security of tenure. Fifteen years later, most states have taken only a few reluctant and farcical weak steps to comply with these directions.

The challenge placed before us by the Hashimpura case goes beyond the concerns addressed by the Supreme Court and provides proof of the deeply embedded institutional biases against Muslims within the police force.

The Hashimpura case is now before the Supreme Court, where the fifteen surviving PAC convicts, have filed bail applications and appeals against conviction.

In Mohalla Hashimpura, the age of the case is marked by the age of Zaibunissa's daughter. In May 1987, Zaibunissa gave birth to a girl, who never met her father, as he fell to the bullets of the PAC on that summer night.

With the passage of time, the baton has passed on to the next generation in Mohalla Hashimpura, who have inherited the tenacious will to pursue justice.

4

PRISONERS, A LAWYER AND THE QUESTION OF LIFE AND PERSONAL LIBERTY

DEEPAN KUMAR SARKAR

Those of us who can take a ride to work and back, step out from the office for a bit of fresh air, visit cafes or buy a plane ticket, take personal liberty for granted. This liberty is so fundamental to everything we do and it comes so easy that we don't realize its value as we go on with our lives. Like we miss the air we breathe only when we are left gasping for it, the value of personal liberty is perhaps best realized by its absence. I encountered that absence, in its manifest form, when I first entered a prison to fulfil the professional obligation of providing legal aid to a prisoner. One visit became many; what started as a professional obligation soon became a personal realization.

I was a law student by chance rather than design. My interests included a range of subjects but definitely steered clear of the universe of long-winded sentences, humourless propositions and seemingly lifeless theoretical ideas. The first two years of studying the law were excruciating.

In the third year, we started reading the Constitution of India and the basis of all the freedoms and rights we enjoy now became apparent. Past and present experiences throughout the world had demonstrated to the framers of the Constitution the necessity of securing certain fundamental freedoms to the people of India and in some cases, all persons situated within the territory of India. These freedoms were enshrined in Part III of the Constitution of India, which was finally adopted in its entirety on and from 26 January 1950.

Some of these freedoms guaranteed as fundamental rights are the right to equality before law, equal protection of the laws within the territory of India (Article 14), the six freedoms[1] of speech and expression, to assemble peacefully and without arms, to form association and unions, to move freely throughout the territory of India and to reside and settle in any part of the country (Article 19[1]), the right to protection in respect of conviction or offences, the right to protection against arrest and detention in certain cases (Article 22) and a most basic right enshrined in Article 21, which solemnly guaranteed that no person shall be deprived of his right to life and of personal liberty except according to procedure established by law. However, none of these freedoms was conceived to be absolute. In other words, the right to freedom of speech and expression could be subjected to reasonable restrictions, which the Legislature could impose by enacting a law in the interests of the sovereignty and integrity of India, the security of the State, public order, decency or morality, or in relation to contempt of court or incitement to an offence, amongst other reasons. Similarly, the fundamental right to life and personal liberty was also fettered by laws which could deprive a person of his life or personal liberty under certain circumstances as long as such a law was reasonable, fair and just.

---

[1] Originally, seven freedoms were conferred, including the Fundamental Right to Property (Article 19[1]{f}). However, the Right to Property was demoted from a Fundamental right to a Constitutional right (Article 300A) by way of the Forty-fourth Amendment to the Constitution of India in 1978.

The first realization that I had upon learning these freedoms was one of empowerment. It was reassuring to know that what Article 21 guaranteed to me was something more than survival or animal existence[2]; it gave me the right to live with human dignity.[3] In fact, all those aspects of my life which would make it meaningful, complete and worth living were constitutionally protected:[4] for instance, my right to food, water, clean environment, education, medical care and shelter.[5] Similarly, a necessary concomitant was my personal liberty. Though, initially interpreted to be mere freedom from physical restraint by incarceration or otherwise,[6] the courts have held it to be pregnant with a variety of rights which make up a person's personal liberty other than those already included under Article 19.[7] Therefore, the term 'personal liberty' is now construed as of the widest amplitude.[8] As a law student, I was enjoying these freedoms as a matter of habit anyway; this knowledge was a validation and hardly anything more.

However, I realized what deprivation of life and personal liberty could mean when I entered a prison as an intern/volunteer for the CHRI. The prison reforms programme was at a nascent stage in the state of West Bengal. Although personnel were limited, the enthusiasm was abundant. My initial task was to assist the CHRI in primarily making prison visits to the Presidency Correctional Home,[9] Alipore Central Correctional

---

[2] *Olga Tellis vs Bombay Corporation* AIR 1986 SC 180 (pr. 33–34).

[3] *Francis Coralie Mullin vs Union Territory Delhi*, Administrator AIR 1981 SC 746 (para 3).

[4] *Maneka Gandhi vs Union of India* AIR 1978 SC 597.

[5] *Chameli Singh vs State of U.P.* (1996) 2 SCC 549 (para 8).

[6] *A. K. Gopalan vs State of Madras* AIR 1950 SC 27.

[7] *District Registrar and Collector vs Canara Bank* (2005) 1 SCC 496.

[8] *State of Maharashtra vs Chandrabhan* AIR 1983 SC 803 (paras 1, 20).

[9] As jails are known in West Bengal and defined as such in Section 2(c) of the West Bengal Correctional Services Act, 1992.

Home and Dum Dum Central Correctional Home, all situated in or around Kolkata. The aim was to identify inmates in these jails who were unable to afford proper legal aid and, thereafter, help them get better access to the criminal justice system. During my first visit to the correctional home, my perception was of confinement and isolation; that access to the jail itself was severely restricted only added to that perception. Initially, we interacted with a few inmates – undertrials, expressing their grievances against their respective legal aid lawyers who were apparently not doing enough to secure their release by obtaining bail. Anxiety was writ large on their faces. That anxiety, which I have seen on several faces since then and with which I have become familiar over time, was a manifestation of desperation caused by the deprivation of personal liberty. The law was suddenly not dry words anymore but etched in flesh and blood for me to assess in human terms.

The first visit led to many more. In West Bengal, jails are called correctional homes. The West Bengal Correctional Services Act, 1992, was at least an etymological, if not substantive, acknowledgement of the gradual shift from a retributive theory of punishment to reformative. A suspected or a convicted wrongdoer would no longer be sent to suffer in prison but to be rehabilitated in a correctional home. Despite positive steps being taken, both in West Bengal and India in general, substantive reform is still at a rudimentary stage.

This brings us to questions about law, crime and imprisonment in jail as a mode of punishment.

In a democratic society, we are governed by the rule of law, which flows from the Constitution of India, as well as certain natural law rights. The rule of law postulates the supremacy of laws as opposed to that of women and men. These laws, shorn of intricacies, may be said to essentially lay down a set of dos and donts and try to give expression to what society at large considers as acceptable or not. Based on these expressions, it seeks to allow what is considered right and punish what is deemed to be wrong. The law being supreme is to be followed by one and all; when it is disobeyed or violated, we have our offender. The offence committed may be a civil wrong or a criminal wrong, or both at the same time. It is usually criminal wrongs that are considered offences against society and that provide for imprisonment as a punishment.

The earlier forms of punishment for conduct which society deemed morally, socially or politically incorrect were purely harsh and corporal. An eye for an eye or a tooth for a tooth was the primitive idea of punishment.[10] With time, the targets of punishment became a mixture of one's body, mind and possession. Whereas monetary fines and dispossession from property was common, corporal punishment was also largely introduced and included various forms of physical torture such as beheading, slaying, whipping, dismembering and beating.[11] Another form of punishment was by way of banishment from society. Initially, imprisonment was perhaps used to confine a person so that he could undergo physical punishment. Gradually, imprisonment itself became the punishment, to keep in isolation those persons from whom society wanted to protect itself.

If one thought that imprisonment is less torturous a punishment as opposed to the other modes mentioned above, one might well be mistaken. Apart from complete physical deprivation or being under the control of others or the threat of physical harm from other inmates or officials, many have described imprisonment to be a 'psychological punishment'.[12]

---

[10] *Hammurabi's Code*, Nos. 25, 195, 196, 197, 198, 199 and 200. Code accessed at https://avalon.law.yale.edu/ancient/hamframe.asp.

[11] Newman 1978, as referred to in the *Philosophy and History of Prison*, Joycelyn M. Pollock.

[12] A. Mickunas, `Philosophical Issues Related to Prison Reform', in J. Murphy and J. Dison eds., *Are Prisons Any Better? Twenty Years of Correctional Reform*, CA: Sage Publications, 1990, p. 78.

Prison attacks the soul, it attacks the heart, the thoughts, the will, the inclinations of the prisoner.[13]

In the early days, the idea of punishment was retributive or deterrent, but the twentieth and twenty-first centuries have seen an overwhelming push to recognize 'reformation of the so-called criminal' as a predominant goal of punishment. The increasing awareness of human rights and strict adherence to rule of law, irrespective of status, have contributed to this development. While keeping the offender outside the confines of society, the idea was to adopt proactive measures and provide an environment inside jails so that the offender emerges reformed and rehabilitated, ready to live harmoniously in society. Hence, the term 'correctional home' as opposed to 'jail'.

A person imprisoned, by virtue of his position, cannot enjoy all his fundamental rights referred to earlier. For instance, he has no freedom of movement and his personal liberty is only ensured in a narrower sense. However, apart from this, India's Constitution confers a number of fundamental rights despite his confinement. This is also in aid of the recognition of an offender as a human being, who may be behind bars but is never beyond justice.

To see what rights he retains even in custody, one may refer to a landmark judgment of the Supreme Court in the case of *Sunil Batra vs Delhi Administration* (II)[14] where it was held that:

> ... convicts are not, by mere reason of the conviction, denuded of all the fundamental rights which they otherwise possess. A compulsion under the authority of law, following upon a conviction, to live in a prison-house entails by its own force the deprivation of fundamental freedoms like the right to move freely throughout the

---

[13] A. Howe, *Punish and Critique: Towards a Feminist Analysis of Penalty*, London: Routledge, 1994, p. 87.

[14] 1980 3 SCC 488 (paras 31 and 42).

> territory of India or the right to 'practise' a profession. A man of profession would thus stand stripped of his right to hold consultations while serving out his sentence. But the Constitution guarantees other freedoms like the right to acquire, hold and dispose of property for the exercise of which incarceration can be no impediment. Likewise, even a convict is entitled to the precious right guaranteed by Article 21 of the Constitution that he shall not be deprived of his life or personal liberty except according to procedure established by law.[15]

The court further held if the prisoner breaks down because of mental torture, psychic pressure or physical infliction beyond the licit limits of lawful imprisonment, the prison administration shall be liable for the excess. No prisoner can be personally subjected to deprivations not necessitated by the fact of incarceration and the sentence of court. All other freedoms belong to him: to read and write; to exercise and recreation; to meditation and chanting; to creative comforts like protection from extreme cold and heat; to freedom from indignities like compulsory nudity, forced sodomy and other unbearable vulgarity; to movement within the prison campus subject to requirements of discipline and security; to the minimal joys of self-expression; and to acquire skills and techniques and all other fundamental rights tailored to the limitations of imprisonment.

There are two classes of inmates: undertrials and convicts. There are persons who have been sent to judicial custody while their trial is underway or awaited. These persons, despite not having been convicted by a court of law are liable to suffer imprisonment in larger public interest for a number of reasons. They are undertrials. The other class comprises convicts, namely, whose offences have been proven in the court and are imprisoned by virtue of the punishment pronounced by the sentencing court.

---

[15] Passage from *D. Bhuvan Mohan Patnaik vs State of A.P.* (1975) 3 SCC 185, 186 (pr.6) affirmed in *Sunil Batra*.

Imprisonment may be of two kinds – simple imprisonment for less severe offences and rigorous imprisonment for heinous crimes where the convict is required to work inside the prison (for remuneration).

My visits to correctional homes mainly entailed going to what is known as the welfare office, headed by a welfare officer who is appointed by the State for the overall welfare of inmates. At the office, I found other persons helping out in paperwork and engaged in various related activities. To my surprise, I was told that they were all convicts. From their general demeanour and manner of interaction, one would find it difficult to distinguish between them and any free man beyond its walls.

In that office, I met and interacted with, for a number of years, an amiable, down-to-earth, cordial and well-read middle-aged man. Yet he was a convict sentenced to lifetime imprisonment for murder. Whether he had reformed himself in custody over the years or whether he was a man whose mind's construction could not be found on his face remains a mystery to me. He seemed to have no regrets in being confined in prison and appeared to have adapted himself well to prison life. Rather, he had many concerns about his fellow inmates, many of which he would address in the welfare office itself. These included drafting prisoners' petitions seeking appointment of legal aid lawyers, seeking details of their respective cases from their lawyers and legal services authorities or articulating the instructions to be given to their counsel by letter before a hearing. Yet, there was another task which he performed rather well: giving hope to his fellow inmates that an early appointment of a lawyer was possible; that things would be all right; that they would surely be exonerated by a court of law; that their concerns inside jail would be taken care of; and that all was not lost. There were others like him too, working in canteens, in gardens, playing sports and staging plays. Some carried on with their studies, obtaining degrees and qualifications. There was a sense of camaraderie within these groups. Sometimes, this was also facilitated by competent yet humane prison officials. These interactions have only made me realize that the freedom to live and think, psychologically, is not always determined by physical confinement. Liberty is not just an idea to be explored through the laws; if there ever was a real-life interplay between rights and their deprivation, this was it.

Then, of course, I have seen despair, especially among undertrials and convicts whose appeals were pending. These were people who refused to come to terms with life in prison and every day was a reminder of the liberty denied to them. For them, jail was hell: the food was never good; the company unbearable; the living arrangements unhygienic. The right to life also inheres in it the right to a speedy trial and access to justice. Sadly, the pendency of cases, lack of infrastructure and protracted trials still plague the judiciary, which in itself, is both victim and (inadvertently) the perpetrator of the inadequacies of an imperfect system.

There was a Mr X who had once approached us for legal assistance. He had been in prison as an undertrial for more than ten years, accused of being in possession of banned narcotic drugs, which if proved, would entail a maximum punishment of twenty years' rigorous imprisonment. His trial was crawling from one date to another without much progress; his co-accused, who was lodged in a jail in another state, had to undertake an inter-state journey and turn up every time the matter was due at the Trial Court in Kolkata. In this logistical quagmire, the case records were lost. The trial had virtually come to a standstill. More than ten years of Mr X's life had been lost. Our frequent interactions with him were a narration of the real-life consequences of rights, if denied. The sheer misery of confinement, that too with a stalled trial, was difficult for him to accept.

We often come across a sentiment: 'He committed a crime, and therefore he deserves it.' But we forget that an offender is a human being too. He has a family; he may have been an offender on the one hand, but also a loving father and a husband on the other. He may have been a good friend to someone in need. Most importantly, one would have to grant this Mr X his innocence till he was proven guilty. Examples like his are many. He had already served more than half the maximum sentence, which he would receive if proven guilty at the end of trial. This is prohibited by the Code of Criminal Procedure, 1973.[16] Even though granting of bail in a narcotics case is somewhat of a rarity, in this case, the bail had become a matter of right. However, his papers were missing and getting relief was a distant hope. In retrospect, it appears that those interviews served to make us look at the human side of even a possible offender and realize that there was a need, not for sympathy, but empathy; not condescension, but concern. Guilt, if proven, must result in punishment. That is the responsibility of the competent court, not for us to hastily judge. Ultimately, though, with all our joint efforts, the records were found, and Mr X got relief after all. After serving twelve years in custody, he was acquitted. In an imperfect world, even with the support of the Constitution, sometimes delayed justice is the best result for which you can settle.

Our general approach to convicts or even accused persons is usually black and white. The society looks at the possible wrongdoer with contempt and perhaps would not even mind depriving him of his basic freedoms. This is often precipitated by the excitable popular media. There is hardly scope for identifying the human element or the other side of this person. Suspicion clouds judgement. The truth, though, may well be different. This may be illustrated by a young convict I met in one of the correctional homes. Mr Y was convicted for rape and was serving out a life term. He was tasked with looking after our well-being during our visits to the welfare office. He was largely the quiet, brooding sort, displaying occasional aggression in the

---

[16] Section 436A of the *Code of Criminal Procedure*, 1973.

course of conversations centred on questions of justice. During one of our visits, he mentioned that his conviction was for rape. He did not deny the allegation and displayed little remorse for his actions. My first impulse was to derive relief from the fact that he was not moving around us in our midst but was incarcerated within those four walls. Subsequently, however, I did get to know that he had a difficult upbringing in a *basti*. He grew up witnessing violence around him and in his family. The mantra he had internalized from his surroundings was that 'might was right'. In his understanding, women were no greater than objects. Therefore, committing rape was nothing out of the ordinary for him. It is only during his stint in jail that he seemed to better realize and understand that society evaluated these acts differently. But he had been hardened by circumstances, locked up in the cocoon of his own perceptions and, therefore, seemed less likely to integrate himself with society at large. So was Mr Y a perpetrator of a heinous crime or a victim of circumstances? Did society grant him an opportunity to be brought up in the way I was? If that had happened, would he have possessed the same inclinations? I don't have answers to these questions. How far a perpetrator should be entitled to rights when he has violated the same of others is a conundrum which is fundamentally difficult to resolve. The debate pertaining to the legality of a death penalty will make this conundrum starkly evident.

However, keeping aside these larger philosophical problems, it is a fact that a person in jail retains with him certain fundamental rights irrespective of the crime he has committed or is accused of committing, and we must endeavour to uphold these rights as much as practicable. The lawyer's role in this process is important. They ought to intervene for their incarcerated client whenever there is a transgression; if their client is physically tortured (the practice, sadly, is not yet obsolete in jails), the lawyer must move court. If the inmate's health is not taken care of, his lawyer must seek justice. Ultimately, the lawyer must diligently defend their client to relieve him from incarceration. An important clarification is necessary here. Contrary to popular belief, to defend an accused in a criminal proceeding, the lawyer does not lie or concoct facts, or at least does not need to. Criminal law stipulates that an offence must be proved beyond reasonable doubt. In light of the evidence available on record and instructions received, the lawyer's task is to demonstrate that their client's guilt has not been proven 'beyond reasonable doubt'. Thereafter, they have to leave it to the court, which shall adjudicate and uphold the cause of justice.

As a former law student and now a lawyer, it is my duty as well to discharge my obligations towards an inmate who may be my client. In my initial days as a volunteer, one pivotal right under Article 21 which inmates were not always fortunate to exercise was access to justice. Article 21, read with Article 39A of our Constitution, guarantees to every inmate the right to obtain legal aid if he is not able to afford a lawyer. In aid of these obligations, the Legal Services Authorities Act, 1987, has been enacted, setting up statutory authorities to provide legal aid. At the time, the incidence of appointment of legal aid lawyers for indigent inmates was rather low. However, with concerted efforts from all stakeholders, the situation has gradually improved across the state. Now, of course, the challenge is not to get a legal aid lawyer but to get a competent one. Efforts are underway to develop oversight mechanisms to enhance the quality of legal aid services. The Supreme Court has also been proactive in recent years and registered a *suo motu* proceeding to look into the conditions of prisons across the country and has passed a number of judgments and orders to mitigate the lacunae in the present system.[17]

---

[17] Writ Petition (Civil) No. 406 OF 2013, 'In re: Inhuman Conditions in 1382 Prisons'.

Just as there can be no exercise of rights without performing the corresponding duties, one never learns to value the essence of freedom unless one has known or seen its deprivation through confinement. By witnessing and continuing to witness what it means to be without liberty, I have only learnt to value it as the most important gift we possess. And, when we learn to value the essence of our freedoms, we could also try to ensure the same for those behind bars. That ought to be the hallmark of a civilized society – where the law is seen, rights are felt, and justice is palpable.[18]

---

[18] I acknowledge the assistance I have received from Md Zeeshanuz Zaman, a fourth-year student at the Department of Law, University of Calcutta. I am grateful to Arunabha Deb, Advocate, for his substantive help and guidance in finalizing the draft. I convey my gratitude for the guidance I have received and continue to receive from Sanjoy Hazarika, International Director, CHRI; Madhurima Dhanuka, Programme Head, Prison Reforms Programme, CHRI and my colleagues and seniors at the CHRI and the High Court of Calcutta. Last but not the least, I'm indebted to Swapna Sarkar, Justice Ruma Pal (Retd), Samaraditya Pal, Avijit Deb, A. K. Mitra and S. N. Mookherjee.

5

THE ROLE OF THE NATIONAL HUMAN RIGHTS COMMISSION IN MONITORING THE RIGHTS OF PRISONERS

Chaman Lal

Prisons in India are generally overcrowded, ill-equipped and harshly managed, depressing places that damage all who are there, including the keepers. They suffer from government neglect and public apathy, and the prisoners' plights are viewed by some as God's way of punishing the sinners. As prisons are populated predominantly by the poor and marginalized, they are not considered worthy of the time, energy and resources needed for their betterment. However, since the 1970s, some improvement has been made in prison conditions and the treatment of prisoners. This was a result of a change in the attitude of the higher judiciary from its earlier 'hands-off' approach to a more sympathetic role in recognizing the prisoners' right to humane treatment and the obligation of the State to reform and rehabilitate them. In a number of revolutionary judgments, the Supreme Court of India has laid stress on the essential dignity of the prisoners and upheld their human rights.

Prison conditions and the treatment of prisoners with regard to their human rights have been a major concern of the NHRC, which was set up under the Protection of the Human Rights Act, 1994. Section 12(c) of the Act, inter-area, mandates the commission to visit jails, study the inmates' living conditions, and make recommendations for improvement. Right from its inception in October 1993, the commission has taken this responsibility with great seriousness and has been discharging the mandatory obligation through jail visits by its members, including the chairperson and its special rapporteurs.

In August 1997, I joined the commission and held the position of coordinator, criminal justice system (CJS) cell, from 2000 to 2007. Besides accompanying the chairperson and other members of the commission to some jails during this period, I made detailed independent visits to fifty-seven prisons in twenty-eight states and the UTs of Delhi and Chandigarh. These cover twenty-two central jails (CJ), seventeen district jails (DJ), five women's jails, five open-air prisons and eight sub-jails.

Following a comprehensive format prescribed by the commission for compiling essential data and holding separate interactions with the convicts and undertrial prisoners (UTPs) to understand their problems and hear their complaints, I would present to the commission a broad picture of the strengths and weaknesses of the prison system with recommendations for improvement in my state-wise reports. Every one of my reports would be considered in the full commission hearing, and approved recommendations were forwarded to the concerned state/UT government. The matter would be pursued thereafter by the joint secretary of the commission to obtain the Action Taken Report (ATR) from the authorities concerned.

The inspection proforma formulated by the commission followed the principles and norms/standards concerning jail conditions set out in the *All-India Jail Reform Committee (Mulla Committee) Report*, 1980–83, and the UN Standard Minimum

Rules for the Treatment of Prisoners (SMRs). The living conditions and the treatment of prisoners are required to be evaluated in light of the fundamental principles under Section 10 of the International Covenant of the Civil and Political Rights (ICCPR), which stipulates that 'all persons under any form of detention or imprisonment shall be treated with humanity consistent with respect for inherent dignity of their human person'.[1]

The rights of prisoners from the observations/directions of the Supreme Court over the years are as follows:

- Right to human dignity, integrity of body and protection against torture or cruel, degrading or inhuman treatment.
- Right to basic needs such as accommodation, food, clothing, bedding, sanitation and hygiene, healthcare, physical exercise and entertainment.
- Right to access to law and speedy trial.
- Right to communication with the outside world and contact with family members and legal counsel.
- Right to reform and rehabilitation for his re-integration in society as a law-abiding citizen capable of making an honest living.

While numbers one to four above are justiciable rights enforceable by courts, the right to reform and rehabilitation is an important obligation of the State with no binding force. A brief description of my observations and recommendations covering the important aspects of the functioning of various prisons during my visits in different states are given below:

[1] 'Body of Principles for the Protection of All Persons under Any Form of Detention or Imprisonment'. Available: https://www.ohchr.org/en/professionalinterest/pages/detentionorimprisonment.aspx.

Basic Needs

Accommodation

In India, the basic right of prisoners to well-lit, ventilated accommodations set out barrack- or cell-wise as per the UN Standard Minimum Rules, also recommended by the Mulla Committee, is found to be violated in most prisons in India because of heavy overcrowding. The CJS cell's analysis of the commission showed that, overall, average occupancy of prisons was 134 per cent from 1 January 2000 to 30 June 2005 with UP, Bihar, Haryana, Chhattisgarh, Jharkhand, Gujarat, Sikkim and Delhi recording over 180 per cent occupancy. In some prisons of Jharkhand, it was found to be ranging from 200 to 500 per cent.

The *National Crime Record Bureau (NCRB) Report*, 2017, showed that the overall occupancy rate of Indian prisons declined from 140 per cent in 2007 to 115 per cent in 2017 with sixteen out of twenty-eight states having occupancy higher than 100 per cent, wherein UP (165 per cent), Chhattisgarh (157 per cent), Delhi (151 per cent) and Sikkim (141 per cent) fared the worst.

As for the fifty-two jails I visited as the special rapporteur from June 2000 to December 2007, as many as sixteen had an occupancy rate of over 150 per cent and ten had more than 200 per cent (Satna [Madhya Pradesh]: 275; Meerut [Uttar Pradesh]: 261; Pathanamthitta [Kerala] 235; Golaghat [Assam]: 229; Udaipur [South Tripura]: 243; Shillong [Meghalaya]: 224; Kollam [Kerala]: 219; Agartala [Tripura]: 205; Chikkaballapur [Karnataka]: 200; and Bangalore [Karnataka]: 208 per cent).

Overcrowding in Indian prisons is a result of the heavy concentration of UTPs and the police's liberal use of powers to make arrests, coupled with the slow pace of trials in courts. The average overall percentage of UTPs during 1 January 2000 to 30 June was 72 per cent, down to 70 per cent in 2005 with seven states (Himachal Pradesh, MP, Tamil Nadu, Chhattisgarh, Rajasthan, Tripura and Assam) bringing it below 60 per cent. The NHRC's regular monitoring and voicing of its concern played a part in this achievement. According to the 2017 NCRB Report, the figure of UTPs was 68 per cent.

A notable feature of the Indian prisons is over-representation of minority/Muslim communities and SC and ST groups in prison population. A 2012 study revealed that even though Muslims constitute 14 per cent of the country's population, they accounted for 21 per cent of the prison population. Figures for SCs and STs are 16.2 per cent (22.4 per cent) and 8.2 per cent (13.3 per cent), respectively.

I recall visiting a sub-jail in Jharkhand, where a barrack authorized with a capacity of thirty was holding ninety-eight prisoners. I asked for a demonstration of their sleeping positions. The constructed scene presented the site of an unreserved coach at the tail end of an express train. The coach, which is generally meant for seventy–eighty people, gets cramped with 200 or even more people, falling over each other while in sitting positions, unable to stretch their legs or turn slightly. At another sub-jail, the superintendent told me candidly that a full night's sleep of seven to eight hours was a luxury beyond the reach of prisoners in his jail who were provided just enough space to lie down in three shifts of four hours each.

In some prisons of Bihar and Jharkhand, a malpractice connected with overcrowding was detected, wherein there were separate wards for the sick and infirm persons. These were relatively less crowded (150–160 per cent occupancy) than the barracks (over 300 per cent). We found a number of perfectly healthy inmates in better clothes sitting in the wards while a much larger number of old, infirm and truly sick prisoners was rotting in the cramped barracks.

Sanitation and Hygiene

Toilets

Against the ideal norm of one toilet for six prisoners as recommended by the Mulla Committee, I would consider 1:10 as acceptable. The data, which was collected from thirty-three out of a total of fifty-seven jails that I had visited, showed that twelve (36 per cent) prisons failed on this count. Some jails had a toilet-to-prisoner ratio of 1:20 or even worse.

Regarding the bathing facilities, I found that the Mulla committee norm of one bathroom for fifteen inmates was being followed in very few prisons – roughly estimated as 20 per cent of the total. However, adequate facilities for bathing in the open were available for male prisoners in most jails. The sanitation and bathing facilities were satisfactory for women prisoners, who constituted around 4 per cent of the prison population.

Food

In all the states, the scale of keeping food separate for labouring and non-labouring prisoners has been laid down. The quantity of food has been worked out on calorie and protein requirements. Inmates were found generally happy with the supply of food. It may be interesting to note that the prisoners invariably gain weight during incarceration. It is explained partly by the quantity of the food they consume, but largely, because of their poor socio-economic profile, they eat more regularly in captivity than in the freedom of their homes. The poor quality of food – half-baked chapatis and watery dal – was a subject of persistent complaints. Shockingly, children up to the age of 5–6 years who were allowed to live with female prisoners were fed out of the normal food supplied to their mothers without a separate authorized scale of food for them. However, we noticed an ad hoc supply of milk and fruits to children in some states. Jharkhand was the first to introduce a separate scale of food for children upon the recommendations of the commission. It is hoped that since the adoption of the Model Jail Manual finalized by the Bureau of Police Research Development (BPRD), this lacuna has been addressed by now.

The mode and manner of serving food to inmates and seating arrangements for meals are a sure test of the recognition of their human dignity. It was found to be disappointing in most jails.

Healthcare

The commission follows the norm laid down by the Mulla committee that all central and district jails must have their own hospitals manned by a sufficient number of medical officers (2 for central jail [CJ]; 1 for district jail [DJ]) with adequate supporting paramedical staff. The sub-jails can be looked after by visiting doctors from the nearest public health centre (PHC). I noticed the following deficiencies during the course of monitoring fifty-seven jails in my visits:

- Only seven out of a total of twelve CJs had a sanctioned strength of two medical officers. The remaining hospitals were functioning with a single doctor.
- The central jail, Dimapur (Nagaland), with an authorized capacity of 600 prisoners was found to have no medical cover of its own. A sole pharmacist was provided to attend to the medical needs of inmates.
- The district jail, Kohima (Nagaland), which houses male prisoners, was only provided weekly joint visits by two lady doctors from the district hospital. One was found routinely absent. The facility was as good as nonexistent.
- Agartala (Tripura) women's jail and the district jail of Udaipur, South Tripura, had no medical setup of their own.
- The open-air jail, Bilaspur (Himachal Pradesh), which had no independent setup of its own, was attached to the sub-jail in Bilaspur for healthcare purposes.

- The district jail of Tonk (Rajasthan), with no medical setup of its own, was being looked after by a doctor, who visited bi-weekly and was paid an honorarium of 100 rupees per month fixed in 1975.

Prisoners with Mental Illness

Incidences of mental illness are a common hazard of prison life. The proportion of mentally ill persons is much higher in prisons than in the general population. Among the fifty-seven that I visited, there was hardly a prison that reported no prisoners suffering from mental illnesses. Their number varied in accordance with the overall quality of the administration.

The commission has been deeply concerned over the plight of mentally ill prisoners and the status of their human rights. Justice Ranganath Misra, the first chairperson of the commission, had written to CMs/administrators of all states/UTs on 10 September 1996, urging them to ensure compliance with the SC directions that no person be admitted to prison on grounds of mental illness and all mentally ill prisoners be sent to mental health institutions. This was reiterated by chairperson J. S. Verma on 7 February 2000.

In my jail visits I used to pay special attention to this issue and identify mentally ill persons requiring outpatient treatment in the jail itself by the visiting psychiatrist or hospitalization in a mental hospital. In a number of jails, I recommended separate wards for such prisoners and periodical visits from the psychiatrist at the government hospital after my visits.

The hospitalization of mentally ill prisoners needs special and sensitive consideration as per the provisions of sections 328 to 339 of the Criminal Procedure Code 1973, for any accused person of unsound mind. The trial of a mentally ill prisoner is suspended because of his inability to defend himself. The progress of his treatment should be monitored regularly, and the court should be kept informed. This critical matter did not receive much attention in most prisons; several mentally ill prisoners admitted to mental health institutions were forgotten and languished with their trial suspended. I brought to the commission's notice a number of cases of mentally ill UTPs in jails/hospitals for periods ranging from twenty-eight to fifty-four years.

I recall three cases of mentally ill UTPs whose murder trials are pending for several years. It was certified more than once that they were not likely to recover and regain their ability to defend themselves. Since they had already suffered more than fourteen years of incarceration and there was no possibility of resumption of their trials, the commission – upon my recommendations – took the unprecedented action of getting their trials quashed. These unfortunate people were doubly stigmatized for their incarceration and mental illness. Feeling strongly about their right to be freed of the stigma of being a prisoner while continuing treatment for mental illness, the commission got some of them discharged and restored to their families.

The case of Lalung Machung of Arunachal Pradesh deserves a specific mention. He was admitted to the mental hospital in Tezpur (Assam) on 14 April 1951 at the age of twenty-three years as a UTP of Guwahati jail u/s 326 IPC. His trial remained suspended and no one took note of his complete recovery; on 9 August 1967, the Board of Visitors declared him fit to defend himself and face his trial. He continued in the hospital quietly, speaking to no one and receiving no visitors until I detected his case during my visit to the Tezpur mental hospital on 31 March 2005. The commission acted promptly on my report and released and restored him to his family on 12 July 2005. He languished as an MI UTP for fifty-four years, including thirty-eight years after being declared cured of mental illness. Justice A. S. Anand, the chairperson, mentioned that this case had broken an earlier record of thirty-four years a UTP had spent languishing in a West Bengal jail.

There is a need to undertake a thorough study of all mentally ill UTPs whose trials are under suspension due to their inability to defend themselves. There may be a few more Lalung Machungs.

Deaths in Prisons

The NHRC, which was set up on 28 September 1993, had issued special instructions regarding custodial deaths and rapes on 14 December 1993. The commission's secretary general wrote to the chief secretary of all states/UTs, requesting them to direct all DMs and superintendents of the police to report to the commission within twenty-four hours of the occurrence of such incidences. The letter mentioned that 'failure to report promptly would give rise to presumption that there was an attempt to suppress the incident'. The postmortem examination and its video filming and magisterial inquiry were made compulsory in every case of death in a police lock-up or jail. These were then to be forwarded to the commission within two months of the incident. Later, following feedback from the states, the requirement of video filming of the Periodical Medical Examination (PME) was restricted to the cases where 'preliminary request by the magistrate raised suspicion of some foul play or a complaint alleging foul play was made to concerned authorities or there was suspicion of foul play'.

The Custodial Death (CD) cell of the commission finds prominent mention in the annual report. In my visits to fifty-seven jails, I had detected as many as thirty-two jail deaths which were not reported to the NHRC. Nine in CJ Ambala, five in DJ Meerut, four in CJ Hyderabad, three each in CJs Dimapur and Agartala, two in DJ Golaghat and one each in CJ Bangalore, DJ Kollam, the open-air prison in Kerala, CJ Jorhat, DJ Kohima and Model Jail Shimla. Overall, this does not present a good picture of the effectiveness of the NHRC in following through on its strongly worded directions.

The jail staff in the N-E States, though aware of their obligations to report to the NHRC, was found wrongly under the impression that a death in a hospital outside the jail is not a custodial death required to be reported to the commission.

We discovered delays in receipt of the detailed report comprising the PME report and video film. If necessary, magisterial inquiry report was noticed in almost all the cases. The jail staff in many states, including senior officials, was found wanting in understanding that the initial preliminary inquest u/s 173 CrPC and magisterial inquiry ordered by the NHRC are separate requirements. The gravity of these observations cannot be questioned. The NHRC does not seem to have taken them with due seriousness.

The commission has also shown little interest to tally its data on prison deaths with the NCRB figures and reconcile the variations, which are fairly wide.

The NHRC has been regularly making public through its annual report, the state-wise incidents of death in police and jail custody. The number of annual prison deaths ranged from 1,300 to 1,800 from 1997 to 2007 when I was the coordinator of CJS Cell. There has not been any significant change in this situation since then. According to the information collected from the NHRC, the average annual death in prison for the last five years (2014–15 to 2018–19) is 1,661. The states considered notorious for prison deaths are Punjab, Maharashtra, MP, Bihar and West Bengal in descending order.

While deaths in police custody are invariably found to have been caused by custodial torture, the deaths in jail are frequently a result of unhygienic living conditions, inadequate and unevenly provided medical facilities, particularly the referral services. In a large number of cases, the cause of death is found to be the failure in providing timely treatment due to negligence on the part of jail staff or corruption. The NHRC must be given credit for examining every reported case thoroughly and awarding compensation to the victim's family and ensuring its actual payment. However, the NHRC has, in my opinion, totally failed in ensuring punishment to the negligent or corrupt jail officials held responsible for these deaths. It has also not shown much interest in dealing with the cases of deaths not reported to it as per the NHRC's directions issued in 1993.

Board of Visitors (BOV)

The jail manuals of all states provide for a Board of Visitors, comprising official and non-official members and headed by the district collector. A properly functioning BOV can play an important role in improving prison conditions by visiting the prisons regularly, reviewing the living conditions and correctional work programmes, hearing the prisoners' grievances and arranging for their redressal by the authorities concerned. I found the BOVs defunct in all the jails I had visited, except those in CJ Jorhat, DJ Golaghat, CJ Bathinda (Punjab) and Central Women's Jail, Delhi. No BOV had ever been constituted in DJ Kohima till November 2007. I am given to understand that things have improved considerably because of NHRC's involvement and commendable efforts of some NGOs, particularly the CHRI, in this area.

Visits of Judicial Authorities

Since prison incarceration means judicial custody, the district/session judge is responsible to ensure proper living conditions, humane treatment of prisoners and expeditious processing of their trials. The jail manuals of all states contain provisions for periodical – monthly in most states – visits to the DJ/SJs of jails in their jurisdiction. Besides ensuring improvement in the management and administration of the prisons, such visits help the judicial authorities understand the problems and hear the grievances of prisoners. I have, in my visits to various jails, clearly observed a positive correlation between the seriousness and regularity of such visits and the efficient working of the jails. I found things distinctly better in the south Indian states, particularly in Tamil Nadu.

Jail Adalats

On 29 November 1999, CJI Justice A. S. Anand had issued directions to all high courts to hold monthly jail adalats (camp courts) for disposal of cases involving petty offenders who are willing to confess their guilt. He reiterated these with an expanded narrative on 1 July 2003 in his capacity as the chairperson of the NHRC. The monitoring of the compliance of these directions formed an important part of my jail visits. I found that the jail adalats were being held regularly with a good disposal rate of petty cases in the Andhra Pradesh, Karnataka and Delhi jails. The system was not seen in operation in the jails of MP, Kerala, Nagaland and Tripura at the time.

Involvement of NGOs

The role of the NGO sector in improvement of prison conditions is being widely accepted as a promising measure of great significance. The NGOs are making valuable contribution in different spheres, such as education, vocational training and placements, recreation and cultural activities, providing legal assistance, counselling on HIV/AIDS, arranging health camps and visits of medical specialists, rehabilitation of prisoners after release and schooling of the children of convicts. I have clearly observed the positive impact of NGOs' association on the overall working and general environment of the prison system.

The women's Central Jail Tihar, State Women Jail Hyderabad, Central Prison Bangalore, CJ Satna (MP) and DJ Mangalore offer good examples of the positive impact of the involvement of NGOs.

In Rajasthan, their involvement was found nominal and totally absent till 2007 in HP, Haryana, Punjab and UP.

Vocational Training and Works Programme

Criminal activity is a function of individual malevolence and social environment. Criminal behaviour is a result of the joint failure of the individual and the society. The society must, therefore, take responsibility for its role in the crime and make attempts to rehabilitate the offender who should not only be willing but also capable of earning an honest living. The jail manuals of all states provide for vocational training (VT) programmes in self-employing trades and occupations in central and district prisons for convicts. Besides imparting the prisoners an ability to lead a law-abiding, self-supporting life after their release, the VT programme aims at inculcating discipline and dignity of labour by enhancing their self-confidence and self-esteem and helping them in rehabilitation and re-integration.

The facilities of the VT programme meant primarily for the convicts can be extended to the consenting UTPs. Although the VT programmes, which are compulsory for convicts undergoing rigorous imprisonment (RI), do not fall in the gamut of Article 23 of the Constitution, which prohibits forced labour, the workers – RI convicts and willing simple imprisonment (SI) convicts and UTPs – are entitled to wages for these works which accord the prisons the status of factories with fences. In the case of *Gujarat vs High court of Gujarat* (1998), the Supreme Court directed all states to constitute wage fixation committees and standardize the wages which must be fair and equitable, keeping in view the minimum wages notified by the government. All the states accordingly raised the prisoners' wages – from the earlier poor scales in the range of ₹1.50 to 6.00 for unskilled work and ₹2.50 to 8.00 for skilled work to the new scales of ₹15 to 30 and ₹20 to 40 respectively and even higher, depending on the minimum wages notified in the state concerned with the stipulation of further periodical revision. The commission has been effectively monitoring the compliance of the directions of the apex court.

The VT facilities were found well established and effectively run in Central Prison Hyderabad, State Women Prison Hyderabad, Central Prison Bangalore, Central Prison Thiruvananthapuram, District Jail Jowai (Meghalaya), Central Jail Agartala, Model Prison Chandigarh, Central Women Prison Delhi, Central Jail Ambala (famous for tent-making), Central Jail Satna and Central Jail Jaipur. These were found functioning poorly in DJ Meerut, CJ Jorhat, DJ Golaghat, CJ Bathinda, DJ Udaipur and South Tripura. No VT facilities were available in DJ Karimnagar (AP), Mangalore (ATA Karnataka), Tonk (Rajasthan), Shillong (Meghalaya), CJ Dimapur and DJ Kohima.

The initiative of the Model Central Jail Shimla (Himachal Pradesh) in allowing a private company – TLG Spectra Vision Ltd – to manufacture KERO electric heaters inside the jail premises by employing eight–ten prisoners, who were paid wages at rates higher than the notified minimum wages, deserves appreciation and replication in other prisons.

The well-established prison factory at Central Jail Jaipur, which runs a number of trades or skills such as spinning, handloom, power loom, carpentry, foundry, dyeing, cane work was found employing 700 prisoners on the day of visit. The Director General Prison, Rajasthan, stated that this unit as well as some more in other prisons were not running at their full capacity (working for eight to ten days a month) because of scarce raw material triggered by paucity of funds. Besides causing a loss of earnings to the employed convicts, this obliterated rigorous imprisonment (RI) into simple imprisonment (SI) for a substantial portion of the prisoners' sentence which, the DG felt amounted to contempt of court. I was disappointed by the commission's reluctance to intervene and set the matter right.

Complaints were heard in a number of prisons running efficient VT programmes about the delay in ordering the upgradation of workers from semi-skilled to skilled category, indicating casualness and arbitrariness in the handling of this matter. A number of working convicts presented before me as accomplished tradesmen were found to be waiting for their elevation from semi-skilled to skilled category for the purpose of payment of wages.

Several cases of non-payment of full wages to the convicts and clearance of their account at the time of release were detected in many prisons. The records revealed outstanding amounts in respect of many prisoners who had left on completion of their sentence without getting their wages and were not likely to make a trip to the jail at their own cost to collect their dues. Huge undisbursed amount, prone to abuse and misappropriation by unscrupulous staff, were noticed in many places (₹4,42,284.56 at CJ Agartala).

Grievances of the UTPs

My jail visits included separate interactions with the UTPs and convicts to understand their problems and hear their grievances. The main grievances of the UTPs recorded in my visit are summarized below:

- ***Non-production of the UTPs before courts due to non-availability of escorts, especially the female escorts:*** In Bihar jails, every UTP missing two–three hearings was found to be quite common. The situation has, since, eased with the introduction of videoconferencing promoted by human rights bodies, including the NHRC. The system had started working efficiently in CJ Bathinda, DJ Sangrur (Punjab), women's jail Hyderabad and several jails in Tamil Nadu.

- ***Non-production of many UTPs before the magistrate despite being taken regularly to the courts:*** The complaint was: 'We are kept sitting in the prison van outside the court but not summoned' – '*Bulawa nahin aata.*'
- ***Delay in the filing of chargesheets within sixty or ninety days as mandated by Section 167 of the CrPC.***
- ***Delay in the framing of charges and commencement of trial:*** this was as long as two years or more in some cases.
- ***No legal aid provided:*** The system was found to be absent in Meghalaya till the first visit of the NHRC in June 2006. The IG Prison, Meghalaya, admitted that eighty-nine out of a total of 117 UTPs in DJ Jowai were facing trial without any legal aid, government or private. It was 80 per cent in DJ Shillong.
- ***Delay in providing free legal aid to the poor litigants:*** While I considered one-month period as reasonable after submission of application, it used to take more than three months in most cases.

The system of legal aid to the poor and indigent accused persons was found to be inefficient in most jails. At some places, especially in the Northeast, the UTPs were not even aware of these facilities as a matter of right. The performance of the legal aid lawyers and the outcome of their cases supported the general belief that the system of free legal aid to the poor was actually meant more for the benefit of mediocre and uninterested lawyers rather than their clients. The direction of the Supreme Court that public-spirited lawyers of above-average calibre should be selected for the job was mostly ignored. There was no arrangement for the training of the lawyers and no requirement for evaluation of their performance. Many UTPs complained about the irregular attendance and indifference on the part of the legal aid lawyers provided to them. They also claimed:

- Slow progress of examination of evidence.
- Non-appearance of the police witnesses, particularly the IO and the medical officer. Enormous efforts were required to secure their presence.
- Inability of the lower courts to abide by the orders of the high court/apex court regarding time-bound trials.
- Non-utilization of powers by lower courts to grant bail, forcing the accused to take the expensive route of approaching the higher courts.
- Failure to avail of the benefit of bail offered by the court due to their inability to furnish sureties. In some jails, more than half of the eligible UTPs were found deprived of the actual benefit of bail for this reason. The directions of the SC that such cases must be considered for grant of bail on personal bond were not seen to have produced any impact on ground.
- Money-oriented bail system and the tendency of lower courts to impose heavy surety. Some extremely poor women UTPs in Tihar jail were ordered to produce surety of the order of ₹50,000 in Narcotic Drugs and Psychotropic Substances Act (NDPS) cases. The aim clearly was to make it impossible for them to exercise their right to bail.
- Pendency of trial due to absconding co-accused and the police's failure to arrest them.
- Delay in pronouncement of judgment after completion of all evidence.
- Transfer of the trial judge without replacement for months after completion of evidence in some cases.

Most of these complaints can be addressed effectively if the jail superintendent realizes their human implications and brings them to the notice of the Delhi State Legal Services Authority (DSLSA), the board of visitors or the visiting judicial authorities.

The following specific cases are examples of the pathetic conditions of UTPs:

- A cycle rickshaw driver and sixteen others involved in a scandal of blood donation were found languishing since June 2001 in DJ Meerut, which was visited on 18 March 2002. The scrutiny of records revealed that two doctors and five paramedical personnel were also arrested and admitted to the same jail in this case. The doctors were released on bail within three to four days and the supporting medical team also managed to get out within a week. The blood donors accused of illegally selling blood, obviously for reasons of poverty, suffered a long incarceration before being released on the NHRC's intervention.
- In a case at DJ Karimnagar (then Andhra Pradesh), which I visited on 4 December 2003, a twenty-year-old boy was found arrested along with his father and uncle u/s 417/506 IPC read with 34 IPC. While the adult accused persons were released on bail, the boy was still in jail at the time of my visit in December 2004 simply because he happened to be hospitalized for some time.
- Two UTPs admitted to DJ Udaipur, South Tripura, who had been transferred from some other jails, were being shown in custody since the date of their admission to this jail without mentioning the period – twenty-six months and eleven months – spent in the previous jails.
- In a tragicomic situation, a UTP told me that his date of hearing had been falling on a Sunday since the beginning of the case. He had apprised the jail officials and some fellow prisoners of this strange occurrence. Everyone would mockingly dismiss his complaint without checking his history ticket. A look at his history ticket revealed that he was really being called for hearing every time on a Sunday.

It took me little time to see that, by accident, the day of the first hearing had been a Sunday. As most UTPs in Bihar and Jharkhand jails used to complain that they returned from the court after being told about the date of next hearing but without actually being produced in front of the magistrate, every date after the first was computed by adding fourteen to the last figure. Understandably, the date of hearing remained Sunday because of the casualness on the part of the court clerk and lack of concern of the jail officials.

Grievances of Convicts

Convicts were found better off in terms of their living conditions and treatment in most jails. Besides having all the human rights except those withdrawn or curtailed by their incarceration, they enjoy certain constitutional and legal rights. They also enjoy the benefits of some concessions and welfare schemes to reform and prepare them for their return to society. The important ones include leave, furlough, parole, remission, transfer to open-air prisons and premature release. I found convicts in most jails aware of their entitlements and vocal in expressing their grievances. I used to focus on the problems and grievances of the convicts undergoing life imprisonment (lifers). The main grievances of those convicts were:

Appeal

Complaints of delay in the disposal of appeals against life imprisonment by the high courts were heard without exception in all jails holding lifers. The average time taken by the high courts in settling these appeals was around five years. It was much longer in the jails of MP and Tripura. Only the Delhi High Court was found taking an average time of two–three years in deciding these appeals.

In a case detected in CJ Agartala (Tripura), a convict stated that he had filed an appeal against his life imprisonment within three months of admission to the jail in September 1999. He was informed by the superintendent after about a year that his petition had been misplaced and could not be forwarded. He submitted a second petition in 2000, and that was also reported as misplaced. As a result, he could not file an appeal against the sentence of LI even after an incarceration of nearly five years when I saw him in June 2004. In a similar case, a lifer in the women's jail in Agartala told me that she could not file an appeal against her sentence as the copy of the judgment, delivered two months after her admission, had been misplaced in the jail office.

A convict in Central Jail Agartala complained that he did not get the benefit of five years being reduced from his sentence as an outcome of the appeal filed in the high court from outside the jail, because he received no intimation about it from his private lawyer.

Set-off Period

Many convicts in the jails of the Northeastern states complained about denial of the benefit of 'set-off' period u/s 428 CrPC, which provides for the counting of the period of detention during investigation and trial towards the sentence of the convict. Twenty-two lifers in DJ Udaipur, South Tripura, and twenty-one in Sub-jail Sonamura (Tripura) complained the set of periods was not mentioned in their judgment orders. The central jail in Dimapur offered a more significant number of such complaints.

Parole

All jail manuals provide for parole, which means temporary suspension of sentence. Most states were found to be liberally administering this measure which aims to promote the smooth return of the prisoner to the community with the ability and desire to live as a law-abiding citizen. The period spent on parole is counted against the sentence except in Andhra Pradesh and Tripura.

Complaints alleging discrimination and arbitrariness in granting parole were received in most jails. Parole is granted after obtaining recommendations from district police/probation officer and the practice varies from state to state.

The Tripura jail manual provides for long-term parole of two or three years, which, some convicts complained was granted to resourceful persons with connections.

In Karnataka jails, parole is granted only after an applicant executes a bond with two sureties for a sum of ₹3,000 each, or deposits ₹6,000 in cash in lieu of such surety. The NHRC can claim small credit for getting it reduced to ₹3,000. In Kerala, the same practice is followed with a bond by the petitioner and two sureties of ₹10,000 each. These provisions obviously limit the parole facility to the prisoners belonging to the well-off sections of society.

The parole provisions of the Assam prison rules, which are applicable to Meghalaya jails, were not seen in operation in DJ Shillong and DJ Jowai. The superintendents admitted that no prisoner had been granted parole in their jails since the formation of the state in 1972 until the commission's first visit in June 2006.

The number of cases in which parole was denied to convicts even after completing ten years or more of imprisonment in Kerala, for lack of favourable police recommendations, was found to be very large. In the open-air jail in Nettukaltheri, a convict who had completed eleven years of imprisonment, including two years in the open-air jail, was refused emergency parole to see his ailing father undergoing treatment in the medical college due to non-receipt of the police report from the district.

Many convicts in Assam jails were denied parole because their family could not manage to get favourable recommendations from the *gaon burha* – the village headman. A lifer transferred from Tejpur to Golaghat jail could not get parole even once because of this transfer. A convict of Golaghat jail was denied parole because his house was located between two villages and none of the two gaon burhas was willing to clear the case.

In the states of North India – Delhi, Punjab and Rajasthan – parole is granted liberally but only on favourable recommendations of the police. Very few complaints were received from the convicts regarding the denial of parole in these states.

Premature Release of Lifers

Observing a lack of uniformity in the criteria for premature release of lifers being followed in various states, the NHRC issued guidelines on the subject in November 1997, which were revised in September 2003 in response to the feedback received from the states.

The SC has clarified that life imprisonment means imprisonment of the convicted person till the natural end of his life. However, the law provides for premature release of the person that can be ordered by the President of India under Article 72 of the Constitution and the state governor under Article 161 and the state government u/s 432 CrPC. The powers of these constitutional functionaries are outside the domain of the commission. The commission's guidelines concern the powers of the state government u/s 432 CrPC which are to be exercised in accordance with the provisions of Section 433 and 433A CrPC. Section 433A CrPC was introduced in December 1978, following the ruling of the Supreme Court that holds that 'a convict undergoing life imprisonment for an offence which carried death sentence also as a punishment, shall not be released prematurely unless he has completed 14 years of actual incarceration without remission'. Before the insertion of this section, the state governments were ordering premature release of lifers without any restrictions on their powers u/s 433 CrPC. The commission came to know from the jail visits that most states, except Andhra Pradesh, Karnataka and Kerala, were ordering premature release of lifers u/s 432 CrPC after they completed incarceration of fourteen years and twenty years with remission.

Maharashtra was found to be following a harsher norm of fourteen years actual imprisonment and twenty to thirty years with remission, depending on the gravity and brutality of the offence for which they had been convicted.

The commission found that in the states of Andhra Pradesh, Karnataka and Kerala, the lifers were being released much before completion of fourteen years actual incarceration in exercise of the powers of the state governor under Article 161 of the Constitution without making use of the powers of the state government u/s 432 of the CrPC. In Andhra Pradesh, the qualifying period for consideration of premature release of a lifer was seven years actual incarceration and ten years with remission. In Karnataka, it was ten years actual for males and five years for female lifers, regardless of the quantum of remission earned. The releases were seen to be ordered on national holidays like Independence Day and Republic Day. For example, in Andhra Pradesh, 602 lifers, including seventy-two of the Central Jail Hyderabad were released on 15 August 2004. In Central Jail Bangalore, sixty-four lifers were released on Republic Day and Independence Day in 2005 and 2006. The Central Prison Bangalore was not holding any lifer who had completed fourteen years of actual incarceration on the day of NHRC team's visit on 25 February 2006. However, there were four lifers belonging to Maharashtra, whose cases had to be decided by the practice being followed in Maharashtra and one ex-army convict sentenced to life imprisonment by General

Court Marshal in 1992 who, in accordance with the practice in army, could be released only under the fourteen-year rule.

The commission held that routine recourse to constitutional provision of Article 161 in these states had nullified the effect of Section 433A CrPC, which was introduced in 1978, following a ruling of the apex court.

The commission's guidelines are based on the imperative of making a distinction between an ordinary case of murder under grave and sudden provocation with no criminal background of the accused and other horrifying crimes, such as murder with dacoity, murder with rape, murder of a child, murder of a public servant on duty and incidents of mass killings by a terrorist. The commission, therefore, laid down the eligibility criteria as fourteen years actual incarceration up to twenty-five years with remission, depending upon the gravity of the offence and the brutality of its execution.

During the course of a one-day workshop conducted at Kolkata for jail superintendents of West Bengal on 5 June 2006, it was learnt that a large number of lifers were languishing in West Bengal jails for over twenty years. The commission asked the state government to furnish full particulars of all the lifers who had completed twenty years actual imprisonment as of 1 June 2006. A list of lifers received from the state government showed that out of sixty, thirty-seven had been in jail for over twenty-two years, including five who had completed twenty-five years. It was learnt that since the Sentence Reviewing Board was not meeting regularly and did not display seriousness about considering all the cases put up before it by the jail department, a number of cases of eligible persons were deferred to the next meeting. In a special drive started by the IG Prison, West Bengal, due to the prompts of the NHRC, a huge backlog of all the lifers eligible under the fourteen-year rule was cleared.

General

Classification of prisoners

The old system of classification of prisoners as A, B, C according to their social and economic status – and addiction to the superior mode of living provided in the prison rules of several states – was struck down by the Supreme Court as unconstitutional in *Prem Shankar Shukla vs the Delhi administration* (1980). The case described it as 'the hangover of the hierarchical social structure hostile to the constitutional ethos'. The SC had recommended its replacement by a system of scientific classification based on age, health, academic and occupational requirements and security needs. I noticed the old system still being followed in Model Central Jail Shimla (September 2003) and CJ Ambala (October 2003). In Model Jail Shimla, I saw a convict, a doctor by profession, undergoing life imprisonment for murdering his wife, being provided a well-furnished separate room with a television set and services of a helper by an ordinary prisoner who was being paid usual wages for this job.

Open-air prisons

My jail visits included visits to open-air jails in six states: Andhra Pradesh (Hyderabad), Karnataka (Koramangala), Himachal Pradesh (Bilaspur), Rajasthan (Jaipur), Assam (Mohindergarh) and Kerala (Nettukaltheri). The open jails that started as agricultural colonies in the 1960s were found to be in a state of neglect and decay. A well-conceived and thoughtfully designed reformative scheme was not being run efficiently to realize its full potential: 49.7 per cent was being utilized; 537 out of total capacity of 1,080. Only Rajasthan, with 87 per cent utilization, offers an inspiring example of the utility of the open-air system, which functions as a half-way home in the transformation of the prisoners' lives and their return to the community.

Compensation to the victim or his family

In the case of *State of Gujarat vs High Court of Gujarat* (Cl 1998, 7SCC 392), the Supreme Court stressed the need to pay compensation to the victim or his family in case of his death by creating a fund through which a certain amount would be deducted from the wages earned by the prisoner. The directions are being followed in some states but not all. Delhi, UP, Bihar, MP and Tamil Nadu had started deductions at various rates (25 per cent to 50 per cent) from the prisoners' wages. However, the actual disbursement of the fund was not seen till 2007. It is relevant to mention a recent development in this matter. The Delhi High Court is looking into the issue of the deductions from the prisoners' wages for payment to victims or their families, which was introduced in 2006. In an affidavit submitted to the high court in November 2019, the jail department admitted that out of a total amount of ₹15 crores collected from the prisoners' wages under rule 96 (8) of the Delhi Prison Rules, 2018, only ₹1 crore has been utilized and ₹14 Crore is lying unspent. Some other high courts have also objected to this measure. It is doubtful if NHRC has taken any notice of the rejection of the Supreme Court order regarding the payment of compensation to the victims by some high courts.

New Prison Legislation

The commission has, right from its inception, stressed the need for new prison legislation in tune with modern thinking on criminology and penology. It endorses the Mulla Committee recommendation for the enactment of a uniform, coordinated prison law for the entire country. In 1996, the commission had drafted a prison bill in light of the International Human Rights instruments and relevant judgments of the Supreme Court. After circulating it amongst the states to elicit their comments, the draft bill was forwarded to the Ministry of Home Affairs,

Government of India, in 1998, for the enactment of a new Prison Act under Article 252 of the Constitution to replace the old act of 1894. The matter does not seem to have been pursued thereafter, although a Model Jail Manual incorporating most of the provisions of the NHRC draft bill has been finalized by the Bureau of Police Research and Development (BPR&D) and forwarded to all states for adoption. As the manual includes the status of the rules of procedure, it needs the legal backing of the new prison act to replace the 1894 Act.

Conclusion

Prisons are the second topmost priority of the NHRC for its mandated objective of protection of human rights. They stand next only to police in terms of the volume of complaints of human rights violations handled by the commission. Effectively playing its role in improving prison conditions and treatment of prisoners, the commission has done commendably well in spreading human rights literacy, generating human rights awareness and compensating the victims of human rights violations. However, prison overcrowding, the root cause of deplorable prison conditions resulting from the congestion of UTPs, persists as a formidable challenge.

The insertion of Section 436A CrPC in 2006 and the constitution of UTP Review Committees in each district, under orders of the SC, do not seem to have made the desired impact on the UTP situation. Enhancing the availability of bail serves little purpose unless the inability of a majority of UTPs to furnish surety is addressed and the money-oriented bail system is changed, as also pointed out by the Law Commission of India.

Medical facilities in prisons remain inadequate and not very efficient. The incidence of death in jail largely due to negligence in providing referral treatment is a common occurrence. While ensuring an award of monetary compensation to the victim's family and its actual payment, the commission has not been effective in enforcing its recommendations regarding the action against the guilty prison personnel.

VT training/programmes are being expanded and upgraded, and wages to workers have been rationalized following the SC directions. Their utilization is, however, still below the installed capacities in most jails.

The commission has been instrumental is reviving the BOV systems with the involvement of some NGOs, particularly the CHRI, in its endeavour. Its efforts to replace the Indian Prison Act, 1894, with a new legislation in tune with modern thinking on crime and punishment are yet to bear fruit.

A complete cure of the evils and afflictions of the prison system demands a consensus among all stakeholders – prisoners, victims, prison staff and society – about its purpose. Only when all of them recognize and respect that the purpose of incarceration is a legitimate balancing between retribution, deterrence and reformation and discard the two extreme positions – prison as a place of punishment or prison as a school of reformation – the system will fulfil its ultimate purpose of serving the cause of justice to prisoners, victims and society at large.

There is something about prison that makes it impossible to transform it into a happy place to live in. Despite elegant infrastructure, progressive legislation, thoughtful application of technology, prisons will always remain unproductive and depressing places. We need to, therefore, think of alternatives to incarceration, such as community service, which has been tried and tested in many progressive democracies. In the meantime, we should ensure full utilization of the available open-air prison facilities and their expansion and upgradation to serve as halfway homes for the return of reformed prisoners to society.

6

DEVELOPMENT OF STRATEGIES FOR CORRECTIONAL TRAINING AT THE REGIONAL INSTITUTE OF CORRECTIONAL ADMINISTRATION, KOLKATA

S. Ramakrishnan

Background

Training is one of the most neglected aspects of prison administration. One of the prime reasons for the poor state of the Jail Training Institute is the non-availability of suitable training staff.

Working in prison takes its toll on the personnel. On the one hand, they are expected to maintain a high level of security and safety, while on the other, they must constantly remember that sooner or later, the prisoners will return to society. Prisons can be a hotbed for tension, with outbursts of violence from prisoners who are resentful of their situation. Language barriers and environmental conditions can also be factors for outbreak of violence. In one of the jails of West Bengal, the detention of a large number of prisoners from Thailand whose language or customs the prison staff were unable to understand and their detention for reasons other than crime, led to violence. Tensions between groups of prisoners can contribute to violence. The victims can be the prison staff as well as other prisoners. Hence, the better trained the staff, the better equipped they can be to identify problems and dangers and to take timely measures to reduce risks.

The Role of a Correctional Officer

The role played by the prison officers is not only complex, but also requires professionalism. The West Bengal Correctional Services Act, 1992, places a lot of responsibility on the staff to ensure a prison is a space for the reformation of a prisoner so that on his release, he can readjust easily into community life. The Act has prescribed various functions for correctional homes. Some of them are:

- To provide correctional treatment to the prisoners to efface from their minds the harmful influence of the anti-social ways of life, and rehabilitate them in society.
- To adopt ways to ensure that a prisoner does not fall prey to the depriving mental attitude, which may make him believe he is lost to society.
- To adopt calculated measures to rouse in the mind of a prisoner a healthy social sense and a sense of abhorrence against the anti-social ways of life.
- To adopt measures to ensure effective aftercare service of the released prisoners.

Hence, the basic philosophy of correctional training must be for developing skills and changing the attitudes of the trainees.

Expectations from Correctional Training Institutions

The UN Nelson Mandela Rules recommend that the prison administration carefully select their staff, since it is their integrity, humanity, professional capacity and persona suitability for the work that the proper administration of prison relies on. They further state that the prison staff must possess an adequate standard of education and should be given the ability and means to carry out their duties professionally. Candidates from different educational backgrounds get through the recruitment examination, though they may not possess the required knowledge and skills to serve in the prison service in a professional way. Therefore, it is compulsory that all prison staff be provided with training tailored to their general and specific responsibilities before starting duty. Only those candidates who successfully pass the theoretical and practical tests at the end of such training should be allowed to enter the prison service.

Unlike the police and the paramilitary forces, where the import is placed on training the personnel, the correctional services have not accorded due consideration to training. While some officers have made efforts to improve the training infrastructure, the successors have generally – knowingly or unknowingly – not given importance to the training institutions. The training capability of an institution greatly depends on the person in charge. Generally, the department does not consider it necessary to post competent officers at the institutions – rather, it directs one of the field officers to take charge of the training institute additionally. The ultimate result is neglect of the institute.

Perhaps, the following observations in a report by a group of training administrators who visited the Warders' Training Institute in Dum Dum, West Bengal, best describe the neglect faced by a training institute due to the indifferent attitude of the head of the prison department:

> In one of the state capitals where a suitable building for training institution has not been provided, we found that half of the building has been handed over to the police

for lodging some sections of its armed men, and the other half was being encroached upon by the public. There was only one classroom and in a part of it, the school sweeper had been made to put up. We also saw that the walls of the training school were full of slogans painted in bold letters by the Jail Staff Association. While the daily hours of training programme were from 0630 to 1230 p.m., the Principal came there every day at 1100 hrs.

Neglect of Training for Prison Officers

Basic and in-service training in the prisons departments is also a major casualty due to the lack of a training institution for correctional officers. The BPR&D designed basic and in-service courses for all levels of prison personnel. Unfortunately, most of the ground level staff has not undergone any in-service training in prisons across the country.

- Training jobs are not considered as important and the jail official are mostly unwilling to be posted to such assignments; thus, most of the posts of the trainers either remain vacant or are manned by officers who have not been 'successful' in the jails.
- The organization is reluctant to post competent officers to the training institutes as the first priority are the organizational matters. It is, therefore, necessary that suitable incentives be given to the jail staff for their posting to training institutions.
- The head of the training institute, invariably, is an officer who is found unfit or incapable of looking after the administration and functioning of the correctional homes. As a result, very often, a senior correctional officer is given the responsibility of looking after the training institute in addition to his administrative and supervisory duties. The result is that the training institute does not get the attention it deserves; hence, they tend to avail the facilities of the

training institute for their day-to-day work – so much so that the staff of the training institute are utilized for the field duties of the officiating head of the training institute.

Birth of the West Bengal Institute of Correctional Administration (WBICA)

In the past, the West Bengal prison officers were deprived of basic induction training – except for a minuscule number privileged with being trained at the Regional Institute of Correctional Administration (RICA), Vellore. Hence, the prison officers of the state had long felt the need for a training institute in the correctional services.

The credit for taking the initiative of setting up a training institute for the prison officers – the WBICA – goes to Shri B. D. Sharma, IPS, the then Director-General of Prisons, West Bengal. The first step was to shift the non-functional Warders' Training Institute from Dum Dum to Medinipur – in the premises set up as a juvenile home.

At the time, I was working at the Bengal Chamber of Commerce and Industry when I was asked to join the efforts of establishing the WBICA at the Warders' Training Institute. I had just finished compiling the revised Code for Correctional Services for West Bengal Prisons (a revision of the old jail code consequent to the enactment of the West Bengal Correctional Services Act) and was happy to be associated with revamping the training of correctional officers.

Development of the WBICA

Establishing an academy for correctional management (after the enactment of the West Bengal Correctional Services Act) necessitated an organization amenable to academic study and research that could be improved by academic analysis.

Unfortunately, many may not subscribe to this expectation as the old practice of training correctional officers was different.

Prison management was earlier seen primarily as an 'order'-based activity. If one knows the jail manual and gets the necessary resources, maintenance of the correctional home/prison is achievable by dint of discipline, exertion and commitment. Thus, jail management was traditionally perceived to be an occupation sustained solely by proper and responsible exercise of governmental authority vested in an individual. There was little emphasis on academically validated professional practices as in medicine, engineering, science – or even in law. Hence, the process of decision-making in prisons is highly subjective and discretionary, leading to frequent allegations of arbitrariness and unjustifiability.

This understanding of the nature of prison management led to the belief that any average individual, without much academic knowledge or capability, could easily be trained into a good prison officer, if he was coached into being highly disciplined and subjected to hierarchical control, vested with authority and provided basic familiarity with law and procedure. With common sense, discipline and authority, anybody, blessed with good luck (which proverbially favours the brave), could function as a good prison officer.

Generally, correctional officers tend to rely on sharing knowledge based on practical experience handed over from generation to generation through prison manuals, peer group instruction, senior–subordinate interactions etc. Hence, while deciding the role expectations of WBICA, there was observed a necessity for the knowledge and skills clearly identified and generally acknowledged as essential for correctional management. There must be an organized attempt to bring together relevant aspects of correctional management from varied streams of knowledge to the WBICA where the academic faculty, practitioners and ideas could interact. Such interactions would benefit all those involved and stimulate further thought, research and development.

Training inputs

It was accepted that the inputs for the initial training of the correctional officers could be divided into three parts: physical fitness and skills, weapon handling etc.; internal departmental practices skills; and academic inputs and academic skills relevant to correctional management, handling of prisoners, vocational services etc. It was also felt that whereas the first two could continue to take place directly under the WBICA, the last category could be organized through guest faculty, experts, NGOs etc. as an academic course run by the WBICA which should be participated in by those joining the correctional services, either during the basic course or specialized or in-service courses.

Development of physical infrastructure

B. D. Sharma, the DG of prisons, realized that expanding or finding a new premises for the WBICA would not get the priority it deserves from the government. Hence, plans for the renovation and remodelling of the Warders' Training Institute at Dum Dum with major repairs to the old building were made while he managed to persuade the government for grants to renovate the building and set up the officers' mess for accommodating the trainees. An old barrack was identified, which was a barrack for women warders and not in use. It was the then Chief Secretary of the state, who during one of his visits to the RICA, gave the sanction for extending the first floor for the officers' mess. It was also during this time that the RICA library was set up with the help of some of our esteemed guest faculty who selected books for it. A warder who was detailed to look after the library was so inspired by the collection of books that he secured a diploma in library sciences. He thus, became eligible to be designated as the Librarian. This in turn inspired the warder looking after the computer centre – he too, in his spare time, acquired proficiency to impart soft skill training at the institute.

Financial resources

Sharma convinced the government that their initial and recurring financial commitment would be kept to the minimum. The decision to depend on visiting faculty, rather than hiring permanent faculty, reduced the financial burden on the government and, at the same time, ensured that the institute would have a choice in selection of the visiting faculty – a list which would be decided by the Board of Control for training.

Unfortunately, the state government has sanctioned honorarium for the correctional institute which is much lower than what is paid at the administrative training institute of the state government – a difference beyond all logic and very difficult to understand.

Board of Control for training

While discussing the system of management for the WBICA, it was decided that a Board of Control for training at the WBICA would be set up to guide and assist the institute in training the correctional officers as envisaged in the West Bengal Correctional Services Act. The board would comprise the head of the Correctional Department with the director/head of the Correctional Training Institute as the Member Secretary.

The Advisory Board would include some of the eminent trainers from the state's training institutes, the head of the Police Training Academy, a member from the judicial service, a representative from the finance department of the state and others who could advise on the institute's effective functioning. In addition, the board would include officers of the rank of superintendent of the central correctional home and a superintendent of a district correctional home (with equal representation of women officers).

Functions of the board

Some of the functions of the Advisory Board were to periodically review the syllabi of the various courses taught at the correctional institute and suggest changes to reflect the needs of training in the light of the changed socioeconomic milieu. The Board of Control, among its other responsibilities, also examined the training methodology, the adequacy of the instructional and other supporting staff of the institute, made recommendations for improvement in the physical training facilities available at the institute and on any other matter relevant to its effectiveness.

Developing the training strategies of the WBICA (later RICA)

During discussions on the administrative set up of the WBICA, it was decided that the director of the institute must have sufficient training experience and competencies in the fields of engagement expected/demanded from a trainer heading an organization – with knowledge on new training methods, new technologies, new ways of building competencies and new expectations of the trainer's competencies and what is demanded by the Correctional Services Act. A competent correctional officer may not necessarily be as competent a trainer – hence, someone with experience in training in a uniformed organization would be the best choice for the post. The visiting faculty would have the knowledge of new training methods, new technologies, new ways of building competencies and new expectations of trainees to bridge the gap between what is perceived as a good set of trainer's competencies and what is demanded by the correctional services.

The West Bengal Institute of Correctional Administration (later upgraded as a Regional Centre for the Eastern and Northeastern

States by the BPR&D) would no doubt be equipped with state-of-the-art articles to enhance the skills of trainees. Since there was a decline in the professional capability of officers being appointed to the correctional services, it was felt that while deciding the training policy of the RICA, the spirit of the correctional services as laid out in the West Bengal Correctional Services Act would be the main guideline for the correctional officers. The importance of impartiality and incorruptibility of administration should have a prominent place so that the correctional officers have the backbone to withstand the pressures of expediency and perform their specific role earnestly.

Training manual

A training manual was developed to provide the guidelines for the training, empowerment and capacity building of the correctional officers. It was expected that the manual would empower trainers to equip and motivate correctional officers to best achieve their goals as laid out in Section 4 of the WB Correctional Services Act.

The approach of the manual was focused on the correctional officer's learning capacity and problem-solving skills as opposed to his or her rote performance capabilities. The objective was that the manual would be an invaluable tool for helping trainees learn to perform their duties and responsibilities in a more efficient, effective and equitable manner. The aim of the manual was to ensure that the training design was flexible, keeping in consideration the requirements of the department and the expectations of the trainees.

Objectives of training for basic courses

The basic objective of any training programme is to prepare the personnel for effective performance of their role in the organization. Traditionally, a great deal of emphasis is laid on the inculcation of knowledge and skills as the twin objective of the training, but they do not get generally make training complete as there is a third and vital objective that needs to be recognized. There is a need to develop, amongst the trainees, an appropriate attitude towards their work and the people with whom they come into contact during the course of their duty. In short, the training for prison officers should aim at developing a trainee's total personality for the effective performance of his tasks in the prison.

Objectives of the in-service training courses

The objective of the training programme was to create awareness amongst the jail officers about various issues pertaining to the jail administration, human rights issues and management concepts which would help improve their functioning capabilities. The intentions of the training programme were:

- To provide information on management principles that would assist a correctional manager in performing their role systematically.
- To encourage the development of skills and formulation and application of policies necessary to transform that information into practical behaviour.
- To encourage and reinforce an ethos of legality and compliance with the human rights standards within jails.
- To equip the correctional administrators with a basic concept of training of their staff for better performance of their roles.

Beneficiaries

The intendent beneficiaries of the training programme were:

Senior officers

- DIGs and Addl. IGs of prisons
- Superintendents of Central and District jails
- Jailors of District and Central jails

Mid-level officers

- Deputy Jailors
- Sub Jailors
- Welfare officers

Training methodology

Prison officers want to know not just 'what the rules are' but also how to do their job effectively within the confines of those rules. There are a number of practical problems that are faced by the prison officers which cannot be ignored while designing the training methodology. Training efforts that ignore either of the areas will probably neither be credible nor effective.

Selecting a training method

Accordingly, participatory training methods were selected to:

- Allow active participation of the learners.
- Help the learners transfer learning experiences from the training to the job situation.
- Provide the learners with the results about their attempts to improve.
- Provide the learners with an opportunity to practise and repeat when needed.
- Motivate the learners to improve their own performance.
- Help learners develop their willingness to adapt.

These criteria indicate that a single training method will not satisfy the objectives of a training programme. A variety of training methods are available to a trainer. The most commonly used methods at the WBICA/RICA included:

- *Instructor presentation:* Under this, the trainer orally presents new information to the trainees, usually through lecture. Instructor presentation may include classroom lecture, seminar, workshop and the like.

- *Group discussion:* The trainer leads the group of trainees in discussing a topic.
- *Demonstration:* The trainer shows the correct steps for completing a task or an example of a correctly completed task.
- *Assigned reading:* The trainer gives the trainees reading assignments that provide new information.
- *Exercise:* The trainer assigns problems to be solved either on paper or in real situations related to the topic of the training activity.
- *Case study:* The trainer gives the trainees information about a situation and directs them to reach a decision or solve a problem concerning the situation.
- *Role play:* Trainees act out a real-life situation in an instructional setting.
- *Field visit and study tour:* Trainees are given the opportunity to observe and interact with the problem being solved or skill being learned.

Elements for Development of Training Programmes

Following are some of the critical elements for developing the overall personality of a correctional officer:

- ***Dealing with an adult learner:*** There is a lot of difference between transferring learning to younger people and to adults. Correctional officers qualify in the civil services examination after postgraduation, and many of them have subsequent job experience too. Hence, it was felt that the following characteristics could not be ignored while designing the courses:
    - » *Adults have different orientation towards education and learning:* The adults' orientation towards life and their broader experience helps them identify what they need to learn.

» *Accumulation of experience:* Experience determines what information will be selected for further attention and how it will be interpreted.
» *Special developmental trends:* Adults pass through developmental phases that are different from those experienced by children. During periods of transition, adults appear receptive to learning related to reassessing personal goals, reasserting themselves as valued members of the organization and society, and reconfirming their self-esteem.
» *Anxiety and ambivalence:* Often, many adults confront learning with mixed feeling and even with fear. Understanding these reactions can help one learn more effectively and assist others to do so.

- ***Designing the Training Programmes at WBICA/RICA:*** Designing and carrying out training activities can be challenging and rewarding; often, ingenuity and imagination play key roles. The satisfaction of gaining or helping impart knowledge to others is also an important task. Hence, it was ensured that in each designed programme, there should be a lot of flexibility, depending on the number, background and learning styles of the participants, the learning environment and other variables. In addition, the trainer was expected to have the following qualities:
» *Empathy*: He should deal with the trainees sensitively.
» *Honesty*: His ability to accept any mistakes in the discussions/training content that may be pointed out by the participants with a positive approach.
» *Patience*: He must be patient with the trainees.
» *Pace*: The participants must not lose interest, nor must they be impatient to jump to the next session.
» *Democracy*: He must be seen as a democratic trainer/facilitator who would not force his/her understanding

on the trainees/participants and should be willing to accept their views as well.

» *Knowledge of the topic*: Being knowledgeable about the subject as well as being aware of the issues with implementation should be reflected in an ability to present such knowledge with cohesion and clarity.
» *Communication skills*: For a facilitator, the command over both verbal and non-verbal communication skills is an important prerequisite.

Training Model: RICA

Based on the above, the following training model was developed for the RICA that shows the different roles the Director of WBICA/RICA was expected to adopt while designing the training programme:

Course Director and Designer	**Organizer of the Training (Director)**
• Designs and adopts the training programme as per the trainees' needs • Knows and uses the principles of adult learning • Introduces adequate training methods • Designs training manuals and reading materials • Develops training methodologies for trainer programmes	*Before Training* • Learns about participants and organization • Prepares reading material • Arranges the training scenario *During Training* Takes care of the trainees and training resources *After Training* Removes sensitive material developed during training

<table>
<tr><td>DG Correctional Services/ Director RICA
• Defines the training situation
• Manages the work of the training group
• Acts towards reaching the training objectives
• Understands and controls the group processes
• Intervenes in difficult situations</td><td>Moderator (External faculty)
• Uses discussion as a training method
• Knows and uses method of leading discussions
• Stimulates engagements of trainees
• Activates the process of sharing experiences</td></tr>
<tr><td>Dep. Faculty/ External Faculty
• Presents the subject
• Makes use of his/her expertise</td><td></td></tr>
<tr><td>Director RICA/ Staff RICA
• Maintains friendly contact with the training group
• Takes care that the trainees feel secure
• Supports trainees in exercises
• Amplifies positive behaviour
• Helps maintain relations between participants</td><td>External and Internal Faculty as Presenter
• Defines the situation of the presentation/training
• Structures the presentation
• Reinforces the interest of the training group
• Takes care of understanding of the presentation
• Inspires, tells stories, uses humour
• Takes care of the language of the presentation
• Uses well-prepared visuals
• Keeps control of the audience</td></tr>
<tr><td>External facilitators
Adapts the training programmes as per the needs of the users.</td><td></td></tr>
</table>

Designing the Training Programme

The training programme for the prison staff at the WBICA/ RICA has been broadly divided into the following stages:

- Pre-design stage
- Design stage
- Post-design stage

Design stage

The following are some of the definitions which form the basics of some of the learning objectives:

Nos.	*Particulars*	*Definition*	*Requirements*
1	Job Specification	Specifies the skills, knowledge and attitude required to carry out the tasks.	Skills and knowledge required for performing his role as per Section 4 of the WB CS Act.
2	Knowledge	Something which the personnel carrying out the task must know.	The knowledge of law correctional management, legal procedures, financial management, office management etc.
3	Skill	An act or series of acts which require practice in order to perform the task proficiently.	Human resource management, financial management, security management, office management etc.
4	Attitude	An individual's feelings about something.	Ensuring meaningful work, making a positive impact and being respected or appreciated in efforts to create ethical norms.

Decision about content

To weigh the specific learning objectives in light of time constraints, it is necessary to differentiate between the following:

What is essential	The conceptual knowledge of subjects relevant with the role and functions of a correctional officer, which would include, among others, the following: • Constitution of India and human rights • Major penal acts • Knowledge of the jail/correctional code • Man management • Security management • Office management • Computer awareness • Gender sensitivity • The state administration setup; district and sub-divisional administrative setup; role of the district magistrate • Basics of criminology, victimology and penology • Theories of crime and delinquent behaviour • Treatment of political prisoners, classification of political prisoners and their entitlements.
What is desirable	• Counselling of prisoners • Basics of handling bombs and explosives • Basics of Right to Information Act

		• Contemporary crimes and crime prevention • Financial management • Recidivism and crime prevention • Gandhian perspective of crime • Neo-classical theories of crime • Sociological theories that mention poverty and unemployment.

Integration of training and learning

At a seminar on penal reform, organized by the RICA, Kolkata, in collaboration with the Penal Reform International (PRI) and the Penal Reform and Justice Association (PRAJA) on 13 December 2013 regarding training reforms, the following points were emphasized:

- Trainers at the correctional training institute have to deal with adult learners. There are certain characteristics which are entirely different and cannot be ignored by a trainer. While few of them doubt their own learning ability, their participation and learning are affected by the need to avoid revealing professional incompetence in public. This is an important factor that affects the trainee in outdoor training.
- The interest of a participant in the training will entirely depend on the reality of the programme. If he/she feels the training has some connection with reality, based on their experience and it can be useful to handle situations in the future, the trainee will take part in the programme. Hence, incorporating reality into the training programme is essential. It can be done by integrating both the teaching and training.
- The methodology of training has to be reviewed and changed. It is important to integrate knowledge and skills – this should not be left exclusively for the practical training.

What is proposed in the learning sequence

While going through the old programmes conducted at the Warders' Training Institute, it was observed that while there was some element of sequence in the learning events, there was no synchronicity between the role expectations of a correctional officer – as laid out in the West Bengal Correctional Services Act – and the skill development as well as the visits/attachments to other organizations.

Hence, in order to sequence the learning and maintain skill development for directly recruited correctional officers, the following methodology had to be adopted:

- The entire training duration would be divided into four phases of training, which will be as per the role expectations laid out in the West Bengal Correctional Services Act.
- The first phases of training would concentrate on the development of basic knowledge/learning and skills essential for a correctional officer; the other requirements would be modelled from the training according to the expectations of the role.
- Each subject would be sequenced as per the responsibilities.
- The attachment/visits to different organizations would include a specific learning objective, either to improve the learning or appreciate the need for subsequent learnings.
- The learning events (indoor training) would have to be sequenced with the outdoor skill development programme.

Accordingly, steps were taken to adopt the 'integrated' or 'concentric' methodology in the basic training programme. Under this, in respect of integrated methodology, all the aspects of a theme are taken up together to focus on problem-solving rather than on memorizing various sections of texts.

Sequencing content

While sequencing the content is a matter of judgement, it was observed that the correct sequencing of the events of training would result in better acceptance of the training. The decisions on sequencing were based on the following:

- How to start on past experience and knowledge – where to start
- How to build up progressively the inputs on skill and knowledge
- How chunks would be used to complement each other in the development of the learning
- Where and when to attempt 'unfreezing' past attitudes
- When and how to include practice, reinforcement, transfer application
- How to maintain variety and interest
- How best to pace the learning.

Deciding the trainers

The primary consideration for the selection of a trainer must be competence along with training skills. The factors to influence the selection of the trainer are:

- Credibility with learners
- Range of experience
- Availability

Post-design stage

Once the design for the course was finalized, the training schedule was documented for the benefit of the participants of the courses at the RICA. The content of the training directive issued to the trainees was as below:

- Objective of the training
- Administrative arrangements
- Syllabus for the course

- Details of various activities for the course
- Block syllabus
- Block timetable
- The weekly training programme

Copies of the training directive were made available to the faculty, trainees, trainers and the administrative machinery.

Evaluation

While implementing the design, the difficulties experienced were recorded. The following system of evaluation of a course was adopted at the RICA:

1	Immediate validation	• Informal discussions • End of the session/learning unit reaction questionnaires – written
2	End-of-term validation	• Informal discussions • Formal verbal reviews – follow-up meetings • Written reports

The Reality Model does not restrict itself to experiences, but a trainee can perceive the training event to prepare for any future roles or for events. If the trainee perceives an event as having little basis in reality, he will not be able to relate the activities with his experience at work. In an article, Don Binstead and Roger Stuart have pointed to three dimensions to reality. They are:

Content reality: The trainee perceives how closely the content of the training event is in accord with the content of his work role.

Content Reality

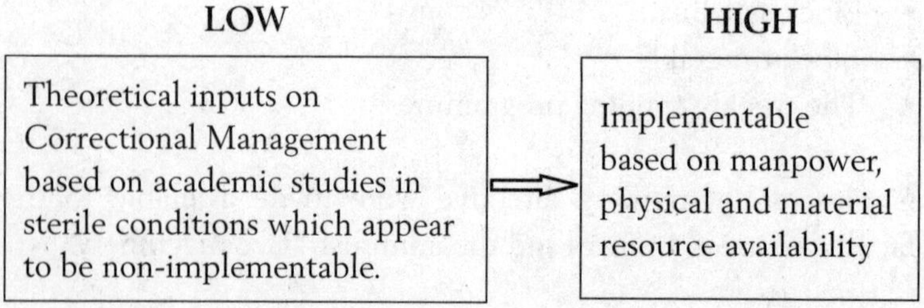

Process reality: The extent of a trainee's engagement in the process can be compared with the processes in his real work. Here, 'process' is used in the behavioural sense which includes human interactions.

Environmental reality: The extent to which the learning environment is perceived as near to the trainee's real-life environment.

The Reality Model

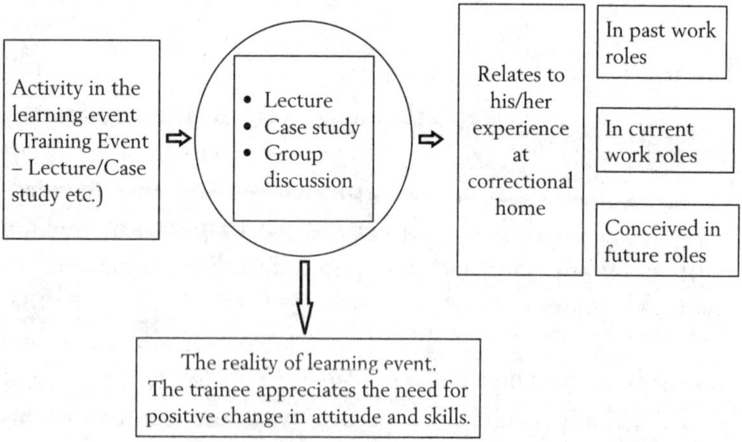

Based on the above strategies, the following Reality Model has been adopted at the WBICA/RICA:

The above model was adopted by integrating the learning event to the work role. This was done by working and learning through any of the following:

- Take the learning event to the job.
- Bring the job to the learning event.
- Provide a range of alternative activities during the training event.
- Change the work situation to match the training event.

In order to acquire practical skills as well as to get acquainted with various aspects of functioning of a correctional home, every trainee is required to undergo a three-day attachment with a correctional home during the course of the basic training. During this attachment, the officer trainees are exposed to the correctional home records, dealing with prisoners, security and other aspects of the functioning of a correctional home. They are expected to appreciate the level of knowledge, skills, understanding, attitudes and behaviour required for effectively discharging their duties at a correctional home.

Other Changes/Development of Training Capsules

- ***Development of sensitivity during the training:*** Developing a strong desire to work with offenders is an asset, and staff members need to be sensitive and aware of the specific needs of the prisoners.
- ***Substance abuse and drug dependency:*** The majority of programmes currently available to offenders address substance abuse and drug dependency. To address this, a combination of treatment with education was developed.
- ***Parenting and childcare:*** Unlike other inmates, the children living in jail are not there due to any delinquent behaviour,

but because their mothers are in jail. The main concerns that parenting and childcare programmes attempt to address are prenatal care, the care and placement of children, visitation policies and custody rights.

- ***Mental health:*** Mental health programmes are designed specifically for the treatment offenders who have cognitive, emotional and/or basic skills challenges.
- ***Educational skills:*** Educational programmes are focused on upgrading education, vocational interest and preparation, résumé writing, employability skills and skills training programmes.
- ***Vocational skills:*** Development of usable/employable skills among offenders.
- ***Additional programmes and issues of female offender programming:*** Abuse and trauma recovery programmes are essential to the treatment of offenders because many of them have suffered a traumatic experience at least once in their lifetime, most having several traumatic experiences.
- ***Training of women correctional officers:*** The strength of women correctional personnel is rapidly growing in strength in the police organization. This is the time to analyse if the training being provided to the women personnel needs some change.
- ***Computer training:*** Adequate numbers of computers have been installed with internet facilities. The trainees will be given an opportunity to learn how to use computers and maintain the correctional home records on the softwares developed by the National Crime Records Bureau etc.
- ***Sensitization for protection of the weaker sections of society:*** The objective of such courses is to generate an awareness amongst the trainees about their responsibilities and obligations towards the weaker sections of the society.

Development of the Outdoor Training Capsules at the WBICA/RICA

Working in a prison is a deeply stressful and demanding profession. Prison officers are required to maintain good health and physical fitness. The outdoor training modules are intended to develop physical fitness, stamina, endurance and certain practical skills, including unarmed combat and weapon training etc. required for the officers to effectively discharge their duties. Another objective is to inculcate in the trainee officers a habit of undertaking regular physical exercise to be able to withstand the strain and stress of a prison job. The components of the drill that help develop personality and bearing and build esprit de corps have been retained.

Most of the trainees on joining are generally physically unfit; many of them are indolent and lazy, and few are in a fit state to undertake with vigour the work required of them. To break the monotony of training, games like volleyball, basketball, football, cricket, hockey etc. are included. The trainee officers are also provided with opportunities to learn individual games including badminton and lawn tennis. The training for unarmed combat and self-defence techniques such as karate have been provided to infuse expertise in self-defence. Sessions on yoga and meditation are also included as part of training for stress management and help them maintain physical and mental harmony. Besides these, certain basic skills training, which are deemed essential for everyone, such as swimming, driving etc are also included.

Physical training has, therefore, been introduced to produce an erudition of activity, alertness and health which will enable a recruit to undertake zealously the duties of his daily life and perform them vigorously without any strain on his system.

The following are some of the issues that received particular attention at the RICA while dealing with adult trainees for the outdoor training programme:

Zero-month training: The stress fracture rates among elder trainees during basic training are more than twice those reported for trainees of a lower age group. Preventing injury to the trainee officers in basic training was re-assessed to reduce injuries like stress fracture, muscular injuries while maintaining the desired improvement in fitness. The concept of achieving certain levels of physical fitness by laying down certain targets was modified. The initial physical problems faced by trainees in reaching arbitrary physical standards and their inability to reach the targets have negative impact on their learning potential.

- The introduction of the 'zero-month' training, during which, more attention is paid on 'breaking-in' the trainee so that he/she is able to achieve a level of physical fitness that would make them feel comfortable during subsequent training. During this period, there is little attention on drills. This period was termed as an indoor intensive training period, where more time was spent on the indoor subjects and the physical 'breaking-in' is done gradually.
- The trainees were encouraged to participate in games like handball where the physical breaking-in of the trainee is gradual, informal and less regimented.

Yoga: Yoga should not be taught as a way of developing physical fitness. It was necessary that this subject be handled as a professional capsule with expertise on the subject. The introduction of yoga during the 'breaking-in period' turned out to be a successful experiment.

Unarmed combat: Unarmed combat develops confidence amongst the correctional personnel while dealing with unruly elements. The objective is to build confidence in the personnel to deal with incidents of high-handed behaviour by criminals and anti-socials lodged in the correctional homes.

Weapons training: The purpose of the use of weapons is defeated if it is conducted under sterilized conditions. In the field, the personnel resort to the use of firearms when all other means of dealing with criminals, anti-social elements etc have failed. When the correctional personnel use the firearm, they do so under tremendous physical and mental stress. Efforts were made for simulating such conditions during the firing practices.

- The evaluation system for testing the capability of a trainee in handling each of the weapons was modified from the practice followed in the police.

Riot drill: Efforts were made to train the correctional personnel in dealing with violence among the prisoners in a correctional home so they can bring the situation under control with the use of minimum force. It must be noted that in incidents of disorder at a correctional home, the correctional staff is often required to handle situations with limited resources.

Instructional practice: Efforts were made to prepare the trainees to supervise on-the-job training of their staff. Each trainee would be required to assume the role of the commander in turn and gain confidence about being able to conduct training for his colleagues.

Guidelines for Outdoor Instructors

It must be emphasized that to avoid making the training irksome, the instructors must endeavour not only to arouse their trainees' interest in their physical fitness, but to train their minds. One of the principal ways of doing this is to avoid making the exercises wearisome by frequent repetition.

On no account must physical training be confused with drills and the less it partakes of the nature of a parade, the better.

The instructor should be clear, concise and patient; he must make allowances for the different capacities of men under training and avoid discouraging them. He must remember that careful individual instruction is the best means of developing the intelligence and, as far as possible, he can teach his men by performing the movements himself. Drills shall be short and frequent to avoid exhaustion; recruits should be advanced progressively from one exercise to another. All motions must be thoroughly mastered before the instruction by numbers ceases.

Yoga should be given emphasis with the objective of developing the habit among officers of doing asanas in their rooms within the limited time at their disposal. Asanas must be selected keeping in mind the duties being performed by correctional personnel and the diseases to which they may be prone.

Injury Management

Suffering an injury can be a terrible and aggravating experience for a trainee. Injuries interrupt training, cause de-conditioning and can be downright discouraging. It often takes trainees months of serious training to merely gain back what was lost to begin with. Many of the injuries that are sustained during outdoor classes are because of the inability of the instructor to understand the reasons and cause for such injuries.

Conclusion

WBICA, upgraded as the Regional Institute of Correctional Administration, has evolved as a centre of excellence in preparing correctional officers to meet the role set for them in the West Bengal Correctional Services Act. With state-of-the-art infrastructure and a scientifically designed curriculum, the training for the correctional officers covers all aspects of correctional management, while also promoting a holistic approach to health, stress control and overall well-being. Growth is a difficult journey for recently established training institutes and, as paradoxical as it sounds, as you grow and add more courses for training, things don't get easier. Growth increases complexity, it doesn't reduce it. Hence, the RICA must be aligned with a mindset for growth.

To achieve this, the director of the institute has an important role to play. Holding dual charge as the director of RICA, he/she is bound to neglect one of their assignments. Training is a basic aspect of any job; hence, the growth will depend on the head of the training institution who must pay enough attention and thought to the process. Only a comprehensive plan to train the correctional officers according to their needs and the alignment of these needs with organizational goals would ensure true progress for the organizations. The director can ensure this using their personality, intelligence, maturity and experience. As a friend, philosopher and guide, he must possess these three-dimensional traits. The director can be a friend by sharing their feelings, opinions and desires with the trainees. They can also be a philosopher by utilizing their intelligence and experience and thereby guiding the trainees as and when time requires. The director can be a guide by supervising and communicating the training plans and policies of the top management and work in tandem to achieve the combined goals.

7

THE WORLD OF PRISONS

SUGANDHA SHANKAR AND SABIKA ABBAS

Locating the Field

A prison is a world of its own. But there is a stark similarity with the outside world. Like society at large, prisons are plagued by the same social, gender, cultural, caste issues, and as such, the problems are also wide-ranging and multifaceted. People from socially and economically vulnerable communities form a large chunk of the prison population. This kaleidoscope of issues often gets buried as people behind bars do not find the avenue to voice their concerns about everyday prison life. Prisons comprise a plethora of problems that need to be brought out through voices from within and the people engaged in criminal justice research.

Statistics gathered from across the world by the World Prison Brief reveal that more than 10.74 million people are held in penal institutions across the world.[1] India, among the countries with a large number of people behind bars, had a prison population of 4,78,600 at the end of 2019.[2] This is 18 per

[1] 'World Prison Population List' (Twelfth Edition), Roy Walmsley, World Prison Brief https://www.prisonstudies.org/sites/default/files/resources/downloads/wppl_12.pdf.

[2] *Prison Statistics India 2019*, National Crime Records Bureau. Available: https://ncrb.gov.in/sites/default/files/PSI-2019-27-08-2020.pdf.

cent more than the actual capacity of Indian prisons. It is also among the countries with the highest rate of pre-trial detention consisting of almost 70 per cent of the total prison population yet to be proven guilty of a crime. Placed at the very bottom of the criminal justice system, prisons are a neglected institution receiving negligible attention from the State.

Being a complex setting, prisons function on two fundamental principles: maximum surveillance and minimal interaction with the outside world. Researchers and civil society organizations often find it hard to get 'access' to the traditionally closed and opaque world of prisons. It may involve layers of formal and informal approvals at different levels in the official hierarchy. Approval from the higher authorities does not necessarily translate into access or cooperation at the level of the prison, and prison officers can block access to prisoners for a variety of motives through a variety of means. Restricted access, coupled with the system's intention to sabotage voices from within, makes this field of research a difficult terrain.

Research in Prisons

Unlike the West, research on prisons in India is yet to emerge in its true form. The opaqueness of the institution leaves little scope to challenge the stigma attached to it, which, in turn, fuels apathy and the creation of stereotypes. Fieldwork in a prison setting makes one realize that it is a process of unlearning, shedding stereotypes and doing away with our assumptions before entering a prison setting as a researcher. While sticking to the methodology, the key is to keep one's approach flexible as every interaction within prison walls brings in a new perspective. From individual tragedies to remorse, from unfathomable sorrow to discovering solace, prison life both fascinates and repels.

Frustrations involved in dealing with difficult participants, inmates and staff might deter others. Yet, the opportunity to conduct meaningful research with far-reaching effects on public policy and the people associated with modern correctional facilities often draw other researchers to the field of penology.[3]

In this chapter, we attempt to bring out insights gathered through fieldwork in and around the prisons of Haryana, Punjab and Karnataka. In-depth interviews with prisoners and prison officials shaped our understanding of their ecosystem. These studies were based on rights-based and action-oriented approaches aimed at highlighting problems faced by inmates as individuals and as a group. This approach also strived to push existing systems to work and to bring about sustained policy-level reforms. The chapter also attempts to bring out the dichotomy between the internal and external worlds, prevailing perceptions and attitudes, and the relationship between the guards and the guarded.

A large section of the prison population is emotionally vulnerable, trying to navigate through a complex criminal justice system. It is possible for a person to be arrested, tried, sentenced and imprisoned without anyone specifically asking how he or she feels about these issues. The research may provide the first opportunity a prisoner has to express himself/herself on these central issues. At the same time, prisoners are also in an excellent position to give a bird's eye view of the criminal justice system. For a researcher, this information is a gold mine. However, interaction with them is an emotionally challenging and complex task and requires a highly sensitive approach. Certain questions that may seem innocuous are highly sensitive and may put forth an unpleasant situation for the researcher and the inmate.

---

[3] Allan L. Patenaude, 'No Promises, But I'm Willing to Listen and Tell What I Hear: Conducting Qualitative Research Among Prison Inmates and Staff', Westminster College, Salt Lake City, *The Prison Journal*, 2004; 84(4_suppl): 69S–91S.

The chapter aims to encourage research in the field, especially in India, to increase the focus on incarceration and life inside the prison. In the absence of a body like the human rights ethics committee and procedural ethics guidelines, as exist in other jurisdictions, the role of a researcher becomes more crucial in the Indian context. It depends on the experience and researchers' professionalism to cope reflexively with issues that arise in the course of the research. This chapter will highlight the plethora of ethical dilemmas that we, as prison researchers, are constantly challenged with, which include negotiating a predominantly male space, ensuring voluntary participation of inmates, maintaining the confidentiality of information, and dealing with presumed expectations of inmates from the researcher. While these ethical issues fall within the broader scope of social science research ethics, they take on a particular form within the closed institution of the prison with a captive, vulnerable population.

Fieldnotes from Behind the Opaque Walls of a Prison

'Madam, aapka destination jail dikha raha hai'

Any researcher who has ever been to the 'field' would relate to the above-mentioned statement. Reaching prisons is often an amusing experience, with cab drivers being confused about why anybody would ever want to go to prison. They would often enquire, '*madam, aapka destination "jail" dikha raha hai?*' (madam, your destination is showing prison?); '*Kya aap sach mein jail ke andar ja rahe ho?*' (Are you really going inside the prison?); '*Kya aap poora din wahin rahoge?*' (Will you stay the whole day inside?). Naturally, the prison is not a place in which one would want to find themselves. As researchers, too, we've faced questions like – but why do you want to help 'criminals'? One of our mentors, who has worked as a prison officer, always says that prisons are considered 'social dustbins'. He often made us think – are all perpetrators behind bars or are all those behind bars perpetrators? If your answer is no, we need to look at prisons with a different lens.

At the outset, prison structures are a reminder of individual tragedy. Think of prisons and what normally comes to mind is a cascade of negative images. As researchers, we can be empathetic with the prison population, but we can never understand what a person goes through upon entering the space for the first time. The complicated admission and search procedures are further overwhelming, mostly consisting of manual frisking and, at times, involving strip or body cavity search. Approaching the institution as researchers, one cannot help but notice every detail starting from the entry point. Of course, our experiences are different from a person who enters the space as a prisoner.

Just after entering, most of the prisons have an administrative space where inmates are received before they enter the main residential complex of a prison. Walls in this area have the capacity and current strength of the prison written on a board or the wall itself with chalk. It mainly includes the number of undertrials, convicts, detenues, persons undergoing rigorous imprisonment (RI) and number of children with mothers in prison. It also provides gender-wise information. Though the law requires the prison to also record the information of the third gender, we have never seen that written on the board/wall at any prison till now.

This space is usually buzzing with prison guards, officials, long-term convicts who help in the offices and inmates (mostly during entry in the morning). Among other things, there is a holder with keys for all the prison locks, a corner for prison staff to hang their coat, spare uniform, bag or notice board; often walls of the admin block have inspirational quotes like 'hate the sin, not the sinner' written on them, trying hard to portray the correctional aspect of prisons.

For a researcher, no prison visit can commence without the initial conversation with the officer-in-charge of the prison. It takes time to achieve their trust and credibility. The purpose of talking to prison officials is also to get broad information about the prison and its functioning as every prison is unique in its own way. While waiting to meet with the officer-in-charge, one may come across the new prisoners who are brought from the court by police escorts.

Since this is the first entry point to the prison, the admission procedure also happens here. Depending upon the number of inmates, the procedure takes time. At times, the inmates have to wait for a couple of hours for their turn before a manual and digital record of their details is registered. To record an identification mark, a person may have to remove their upper clothing in front of everyone present in the room. While the staff may not heed much attention to the inmate, it can be a humiliating experience. In the prison, a woman official called the name of an already intimidated new entrant rudely and made him turn around using the force of a *lathi*. With several new admissions taking place every day, this process has become a mechanical exercise, wherein not much thought is given to upholding the privacy and dignity of an inmate or even considering the inmate a human to start with. For the officials too, this is a tedious exercise as, due to the existing staff vacancies, only one or two prison warders are there to manually frisk all the new inmates.

Other than these attitudinal issues, one can also observe the potential legal lapses during the admission procedure. For instance, in one of the prisons, a child who looked much younger than eighteen was admitted to prison because his age was mentioned as nineteen years on the warrant. Neither the prison official reviewing the warrant raised a query nor the police escort seemed to care who had brought the child to prison. In such a situation, if the prison official does not agree to admit the person, the police escort would have to take the child back to the court to initiate the process of determination of age and, in the meantime, keep him in a juvenile home. This example shows how sensitive and critical the role of a prison official is right from the time a person enters the prison.

As a researcher out on the field, one can witness the busiest time of prison if s/he reaches the prison before 9 a.m. It involves sending a prisoner to the respective court to attend his/her hearing and requires coordination among the prison and police officials. Around this time, a barrage of police escorts and vehicles wait to ferry prisoners to court. Ironically, while the term 'escort' means 'accompanying a person', prisoners are often tied, in a herd, with a rope, much like cattle. The convenience of the system often comes at the cost of the dignity of the individual and this is visible in everyday prison life.

'Sab prisoners ke bare mein sochte hain, humare bare mein koi nahin sochta'

Depending on the category of prison, the position incumbent may be a superintendent or a deputy superintendent or any other officer in-charge. While some prison heads are liberal with the idea of research on prisons, a few complain. We often get to hear, '*Sab prisoners ke bare mein sochte hain, humare bare mein koi nahin sochta*' (Everyone thinks about prisoners, no one cares about us). These statements stem from the fact that in almost all prisons, the officials are overworked and dispirited. This has also got to do with existing State apathy for prisons, as it lies almost at the bottom of the criminal justice system. The prison staff has to constantly navigate this apathy and keep the work going. Managing hundreds of inmates with limited staff capacity is no joke.

That 'first impression is the last impression' holds true in the world of prisons. Establishing rapport and trust may be affected by the age and gender of an interviewer which may elicit different reactions from prison officers prisoners or they may share a distrust for external researchers as they cannot control their findings. Prison officers may also delay the researcher's entry into the prison; or restrict access to information; or attempt to bias researchers against particular prisoners through comments made about them.[4]

As researchers, effort must be made to encourage staff to share their challenges, to listen without bias and to keep oneself in a neutral zone in order to understand myriad perspectives. While we often find annoyance, sarcasm, exhaustion, impatience, discontent in these conversations, the officials also recognize that they are duty holders and their service requires them to do certain tasks with utmost professionalism and accountability.

The prison staff also work with limited infrastructure in cramped rooms with piles of files and overloaded classic aluminium file cabinets. At present, very few prisons, which are newly built, have adequate infrastructure. Understaffing is a significant problem that directly impacts their mental well-being. A prison officer, who worked with two warders in his office, once told us, 'in my prison, I'm the superintendent, I'm the accountant, I'm the manager, I'm the stocks-keeper, and I'm also the driver.' With little family time and almost no social life, burnout is bound to befall the officers. To overcome this, we often see convicts pitching in to do office work. These are convicts with suitable skills, serving long-term sentences, who have established trust over the years. It is encouraging to see the trust bestowed upon these convict officers or warders, as they are known in some states, by prison officials.

'Kaun vakil, kaun judge, sab to kale coat wale hain'

The women's enclosure is usually just separate smaller sections in predominantly male-only jails. It generally consists of a

[4] James B. Waldram, 'Anthropology in Prison: Negotiating Consent and Accountability with a "Captured" Population', *Human Organization*, Vol. 57, No. 2, Society for Applied Anthropology, 1998, pp. 238–44.

few barracks[5] subject to a fewer number of women prisoners. Though it may have a children's crèche, women prisoners do not have access to the facilities available in the men's section like the common playground, places of worship, library, kitchen, hospital, legal aid clinic etc. There are very few prisons where there is proper segregation between undertrials and convicts in women enclosures owing to the inadequate space. The atmosphere is emotionally charged, and at times, chaotic and loud. In our experience, the visit to a women's section is most heart-wrenching, possibly as we can relate to being a woman or maybe because the institution's apathy towards the special needs of women is quite evident. However, greater bonding among women is observed where children are staying with their mothers[6] due to the collective caregiving towards the children.

What makes women more vulnerable than men? The dual vulnerability of women inmates is visible from the fact that they are living in a prison inside a prison. Interaction with many women inmates threw light on the ostracization and victimization faced by them in society. Society's expectations from a woman are so high that stepping into a jail leaves a life-long taboo on them, even after being eventually acquitted. So much so that their family does not visit them as often, does not allow a child to meet the mother, justifying it with negative influence on a child's development, or at times, cuts all ties and leaves them at the mercy of fate. Fellow women prisoners and officials often guide and support the new entrants in the absence of an official counsellor and help them adjust to their new life.

Lack of awareness about one's own body, needs and rights is also common among many women prisoners. Experiencing menstruation in a closed, crowded space away from the

---

[5] A barrack is a big room where prisoners are lodged in a big group. Depending on the size of the barrack, it may lodge ten to fifty inmates.

[6] Children up to the age of six years are allowed to stay with their mother in prisons.

comforts of the home can also be stressful. All over the world, women account for almost two-thirds (496 million) of illiterate adults worldwide. In India, 68 per cent of illiterate adults are women. Illiteracy and lack of knowledge about legal procedures are common among women inmates. One incident that keeps coming back to mind is when an old woman could not tell us anything about her case or lawyer. When asked if she had ever seen or met her lawyer in court, she said, '*kaun vakil, kaun judge, sab to kale coat wale hain, mujhe na pata mera kaun sa*' (All I can see are people in a black coat, I do not know who is my lawyer or judge).

There were also situations where we felt helpless. We came across a unique situation in a central prison where a woman doctor, who was also the medical officer in prison, stopped going to the women's section due to the unruly behaviour of inmates. In another prison, where a women's enclosure was limited to a big room and a small backyard, a mother of a three-month-old girl child suffered from severe depression, and fellow inmates had to save the child from the brunt of her mother's anger. One can document, try to understand the issue, approach authorities for some relief, but cannot find a solution to every problem.

Since prisons predominantly house male inmates, their residential area is much bigger than that of women inmates and forms almost all of the inside of a prison. Though undertrials and convicts stay in separate barracks, the design of a prison does not generally allow to maintain strict segregation as required under the law, between the first-time and repeat offenders or young and old. Indian prisons have barracks and wards, and few cells. It essentially means that one has to get used to staying with unknown persons, no privacy and solitude. There is no assigned place to keep belongings, and one has to hang their clothes and other items in handbags. It is ironic that inside these barracks, everything works based on trust among individuals who are distrusted by society. Everyone has to adjust and alter their way of life. Those who don't or habitually cannot are considered as the 'troublemakers', who may be punished. The punishment, depending upon the severity of the act committed, ranges from being shifted to a cell/isolation ward or can even be a jail transfer/relocation to another jail.

'Aap to do din aake chale jaoge, phir kaun puchega'

Every prison has countless stories. Interaction with inmates brings the researcher closer to such stories to understand the health of the prison and its inhabitants. During one such visit to a barrack, we found a short, frail man sitting in a corner and talking to himself in a hushed voice. On being asked if he wanted to share something, he started crying loudly and further moved to the corner as if he was scared. The fellow inmates said he had allegedly murdered his wife by poisoning her food. The incident had such an impact that he stopped eating. He often hallucinated that his wife was coming to kill him. It may be an extreme example, but the stories of all those in prison are grief-stricken, heartbroken, full of pain, distress and anguish, which may turn fatalistic.

Ensuring mental healthcare experts and improving facilities in prisons are the needs of the hour for both prisoners and prison officials. While knowing these stories leaves a lasting impression on the minds of a researcher, it is even more challenging for prison officials who are surrounded by them day in and out. To be able to withdraw oneself and think objectively and optimistically could be achieved through regular training programmes. While the state must ensure regular training of staff, honing their skills and keeping them abreast of developments across the world, there is a lack of meaningful opportunities to do so.

Broadly, our research focused on assessing the status of implementation of the various standards laid out in the law. In simple terms, *what's on paper* vs *what's on the ground*. Guided by life and liberty as paramount, we examine whether every prisoner has access to a lawyer; whether they are taken to court on due dates; if any person is below eighteen years of age; do family/friends come to meet them; is anyone facing language barriers as they belong to a different state or a different country; if anyone requires any medical attention; if any undertrial has been in prison for more than two years; if appeals are filed by convicts, whether they get an opportunity to communicate with their lawyer and so forth. Based on assessment of the vulnerability of inmates in these areas, we select a few and conduct detailed interviews with them.

Generally, maintaining privacy and confidentiality is the foremost part of any ethical research study involving prisoners. It comes under question in an action-based study like ours, where the authorized functionaries expect us to bring the concerns of individual prisoners to the forefront. Prison officers often reveal that prisoners do not trust them and, therefore, do not share their problems the way they confide in us, the researchers. It may be genuine concern on the part of prison officials. However, what is important at this juncture for any researcher is to highlight issues faced by inmates collectively, in front of the authorities, without compromising the identity of the inmates.

Certain ethical concerns still loom large. First among those is informed consent, ensuring that the setting permits the process of informed consent and refusal. Second, even if there is informed consent, the fear of repercussions always exists. For example, once a group of inmates was transferred to another prison as punishment for simply speaking to us. They were allegedly even denied food. Third, privacy is much more challenging to ensure within a correctional setting. In prison, everyone sees who moves where and can speculate on the actions of one another.

Interaction with inmates is a dynamic activity. Some inmates do not participate in the research as they fear that the information they may provide will not be treated confidentially. They see the research and researchers to be part of the system, or somehow in collusion with the prison administration. However, the majority appear to welcome the opportunity to talk to someone from outside the prison system. Our approach has been to negotiate private interviewing space to interact with inmates. It is crucial to build confidence among prisoners regarding confidentiality and ensure that the research is independent of any confluence or fear of being overheard by the prison staff as the prisoner may disclose sensitive information.

The motivation for prisoners to participate in a research study emanates from the idea of hoping to gain some advantage or tangible benefit in their personal case. Prisoners may have unrealistic expectations of what research can deliver. Therefore, as part of the informed consent discussion, it is important not to raise hopes where the required outcome cannot be delivered. In our own evaluation research, we advise prisoners that what we can offer is a fair representation of prisoners' views in any report we write, but stress that while we can make recommendations for change, it is others who decide whether or not recommended changes will be accepted and implemented.[7]

The fluid exchange of knowledge and emotions is continuous as the researcher and his or her research participants trade the roles of the interviewer, listener, observer and back again throughout the research.[8] Such exchanges occur as the result of a rapport being established and maintained between the parties and often blurs the line between research and counselling. Whilst the research may not intend to provide a therapeutic outlet, the non-judgmental state of the researcher may provide conducive conditions for the person to reflect on matters of deep relevance.[9]

---

[7] Lynne Roberts and David Indermaur, *The Ethics of Research with Prisoners*, Current Issues in Criminal Justice, 2008, 19:3, pp. 309–326.

[8] Patenaude, 'No Promises', *The Prison Journal*, 2004: 84: 69S–91S.

[9] Roberts and Indermaur, *The Ethics of Research with Prisoners.*

Being able to interact in the local language is a must for the researcher. Further, drawing questions with slangs or jargons used within the realm of the criminal justice system also helps the prisoner open up to speak freely with the researcher. These jargons would differ from state to state. Illustratively, in Karnataka, a visit by a family member is called '*beti*' (it is the Kannada word for meeting); if an inmate has faced ill-treatment or torture in police custody, it called '*police ne work kiya*' (the police 'worked' on the person); the common term used for parole is '*raja*' (means holiday in Kannada); for an isolation ward, the term used is '*andheri*'; and for the central office inside the prison complex is called 'tower' which in northern states is called a '*chakkar*' (means a roundabout) or a '*deori*'.

Limitations of approaching the field are clear from the words of one of the inmates who said to us, '*aap to do din aake chale jaoge, phir kaun puchega*' (you will visit for two days, then who will help us?). As a matter of practice, we explain to the inmate the purpose of the interview and what are the limitations of the study. Still, expectations are bound to rise as ultimately, all an inmate wants is to get out of prison. The other side of the coin is self-expectation and the feeling of not being able to help. Guilt and regret are constant companions of a researcher. They may also need to make a judgement about reporting where there is potential for harm to an individual. These dilemmas give a deeper context to the harm–benefit calculus through which the relative value of research needs to be judged.[10] Therefore, predicaments could be many, and one has to handle them consciously and objectively without compromising the principles of research.

'Kya kuch kabhi badlega'

On paper, we realize that the familiar dicta 'justice delayed is justice denied' and 'bail, not jail' are often held out as the bulwarks of a fair trial; however, the profile of the prison

[10] Ibid.

population gives a contrary picture to these dicta. Interactions with inmates highlight illegalities and malpractices that are so deep-rooted that we often wonder if our research would even create a dent in this mammoth system, '*kya kuch kabhi badlega*' (will anything ever change?)

This reminds one of the words of Justice P. N. Bhagwati:

> It is high time that the public conscience is awakened and the government as well as the judiciary begins to realise that in the dark cells of our prisons there are a large number of men and women who are waiting patiently, impatiently perhaps, but in vain, for justice – a commodity which is tragically beyond their reach and grasp. Law has become for them an instrument of injustice and they are helpless and despairing victims of the callousness of the legal and judicial system. The time has come when the legal and judicial system has to be revamped and restructured so that such injustices do not occur and disfigure the fair and otherwise luminous face of our nascent democracy.

It brings us back to the question that we had raised in the beginning – are all perpetrators of law behind bars or are all those behind bars perpetrators of the law? There are good reasons to think prisons might prevent crime. The experience of imprisonment could deter someone from committing crimes to avoid prison in the future. Prison might provide opportunities for rehabilitation. And, at the very least, someone who is in prison cannot commit a crime in the community, an effect criminologists call 'incapacitation'.

Yet there are also good reasons to believe that prisons might actually increase crime. The harsh prison environment could exacerbate mental health problems, make people more prone to aggression, or make them cynical and distrustful of the legal system. Prisons could isolate prisoners from friends and family who might help them find jobs eventually. Or prisoners may learn from other prisoners how to be better criminals.

An obligation of the researcher is to accurately report what is learned. Our research has brought out the realities of prison life, intending to highlight existing issues in prison settings along with recommending a sustainable systemic change. Through this, we work towards the implementation of the recommendations along with assisting the prison official in fulfilling their mandate most effectively, in the spirit of the law. With this aim, we hope to continue our research and further push the system to address systemic issues in a sustainable manner.

8

LIFE IN DETENTION CENTRES[1]

Sangeeta Barooah Pisharoty

In December 2017, I interviewed a few people, mainly women belonging to both Hindu and Muslim communities of East Bengal origin, who were released from detention centres after winning their cases in the high court. I was collating first-person accounts for a video report[2] for *The Wire*, detailing the ordeal they had undergone after receiving a legal notice as a suspected foreigner, and the conditions at the detention centres. Since the jail manual is not followed fully, they were barred from working inside the jails in lieu of wages, not granted parole; the state didn't provide them any free legal help. I also chanced upon a pattern – while all of them had a hand-to-mouth existence, most of the women I met were either widows without children or whose husbands had left them. They had no immediate family, rather a man in the family, who would run around and fight their cases. However, their extended families did come to their rescue.

All the detainees complained of bad quality food forcing them to resort to hunger strikes inside the centres. Families

[1] Excerpted from *Assam: The Accord, the Discord* by Sangeeta Barooah Pisharoty, Gurgaon: Penguin Random House India, 2019.

[2] *The Wire*, 18 January 2018. https://www.youtube.com/ watch?v=c4R AXm96CWI.

of some detainees visited them when they could, with rice, pulses, vegetables, fruits, and so on as per their financial ability. Family members claimed to have bribed jail guards to meet the detainees for longer than the stipulated time. A small hall would house at least fifty women, who would each get a mattress to lie on the floor. Many had either sold their farming land or mortgaged it in lieu of loans to fight the cases of their family members. Some had sold pairs of cows used to till their farming land; some whatever little gold they had; some had even sought public donations to pay lawyers' fees.

Those I interviewed spoke of women giving birth in detention; about children of the detainee women taken out by jail authorities to primary schools nearby; about sharing space with women in the Kokrajhar detention centre whose husbands were in the Goalpara centre, meant for declared male foreigners.

Many such couples had no contact with each other for a long time. In August 2015, Speaker Pranab Gogoi asked the state government to seek legal opinion on allegations of inhuman conditions in detention camps, raised by AIUDF MLAs in the assembly. But no concrete follow-up was done.

In January 2018, rights activist Harsh Mander surveyed the Goalpara and Kokrajhar detention centres for a report sponsored by the National Human Rights Commission (NHRC) where Mander then served as special monitor for minorities. On 22, 23 and 24 January, he met jail authorities, district officials and several detainees to understand individual cases.

Mander's report noted, 'The mission was informed by officials that they are not aware of any specific guidelines or instructions from the central or state government to guide the treatment and rights of the detainees … When we spoke to senior officials of the Assam state government, they too clarified that the legal status and rights of the detainees would have to be defined by the central government, and until then they have no option except to treat them in the way they treat jail convicts.'[3]

Significantly, the report quoted a police officer admitting to Mander's team that each unit of the border police is given a monthly target of filing six cases of suspected foreigners.[4] The report listed a few recommendations, including providing legal aid to detainees on the basis of the United Nations High Commissioner for Refugees (UNHCR) detention guidelines, housing detainees in the same districts as their families, facilitation for recreation, work and parole, and ensuring that officials follow due process and inform detainees about their rights. In June 2018, Mander resigned from his post accusing the NHRC of 'continued silence' over his report and also 'encounter killings targeting minorities in Uttar Pradesh and Haryana'.[5]

Meanwhile, life continues in the detention centres as usual. On a weekday, the one in Goalpara town – the first one to come up in 2009 – is crowded with detainee families. There is a distance of about five feet between the detainees and their family members, separated by an iron grill. Food items from the families are handed over to a policeman, usually standing just behind the grill, to pass on to the detainees. Some detainees could be seen holding the bars of the grill, crying; some others

---

[3] Page 2 of the report titled 'NHRC Mission to Assam's Detention Centres from 22 to 24 January, 2018'. The NHRC didn't release the report upon which Harsh Mander put it in public domain in June 2018. The full report can be accessed at https://www.deccanherald.com/national/top-national-stories/harsh-manders-full-report-nhrc-678127.html.

[4] The last page of the report named Louis Aind, DCP, crime, Guwahati, earlier in charge of border police unit, admitting 'that a monthly target of six reference cases from each border unit was given to the police'. Available: https://www.deccanherald.com/national/top-national-stories/harsh-manders-full-report-nhrc-678127.html.

[5] 'Harsh Mander's Full Report to NHRC', *Deccan Herald*, 30 June 2018. Available: https://www.deccanherald.com/national/top-national-stories/harsh-manders-full-report-nhrc-678127.html.

engaged with family members in conversation about the progress or lack of it of their cases. When I visited the Goalpara detention centre a few days before the final draft NRC was to be published, it was disturbing to see the crowd there juxtaposed against the DC's office, just opposite to it and where the NRC update process was on in full swing.

Besides the Goalpara detention centre, there are five others, all housed within district jails – in Kokrajhar, Jorhat, Dibrugarh, Tezpur and Silchar. The idea dawned on the Gogoi government after multiple police complaints that nearly half a lakh people had disappeared after they were declared foreigners by the tribunals. Even if they took them into custody, it was no more possible to push them across the border. A news report in *The Wire* published in February 2018 said:

> Between 50,000–52,000 declared foreigners are missing in Assam as of November 2017. This is out of a total 93,000-plus people who have been declared as foreigners by the tribunals in the state since 1985,' says R.M. Singh, director general of the Assam Border Police Organisation. This figure included investigations into the list of D-voters put forward by the EC as well as cases initiated by the border police on suspicion.[6]

Dismissing a case challenging an FT court order in 2011, the Gauhati High Court directed the state police to put persons declared foreigners by tribunals in detention centres so they couldn't go missing.[7] Ironically, according to some state Congress insiders, the idea to set up these detention centres was the

---

[6] Soumyajit Saha, 'Detained until Deported: Thousands Declared "Foreigners" in Assam Wait in Limbo', *The Wire*, 10 February 2018. Available: https://thewire.in/featured/detained-deported-thousands-declared-foreigners-assam-wait-limbo.

[7] Writ petition No. 242 of 2011 at Gauhati High Court, *Anwar Ali and Ors versus state of Assam*. The full judgement can be accessed at http://ghconline.gov.in/Judgment/WPC2422011.pdf.

brainchild of a minority community minister in the Gogoi government. The minister, who had a law degree, apparently visited a detention centre (Immigration Removal Centre) during a tour of the United Kingdom and brought home the idea. In 2011, to respond to the Gauhati High Court directive and then in 2014, on setting up 100 FTs, a decision had to be taken by the state government to enhance the number of such centres. While the Goalpara one initially housed both men and women, women were later shifted to the Kokrajhar centre. Some centres house both men and women in separate enclosures. Gogoi told me in early November 2018, 'With the push-back system gone, the court order and a central directive to dispose off the pending cases as quickly as possible, there was no option but to think up a temporary arrangement. With no treaty between the two nations, it fell on the state government to do something. Where would one put such a lot of people declared foreigners by the tribunals?'[8]

On hitting upon such an immediate solution, the state border police went about rounding up those declared 'foreigners' by the tribunals. Some media reports spoke of such people slipping out of home at night to sleep elsewhere fearing police visits in the middle of the night. At present, there are reportedly about 1,000–1,200 detainees, out of which about 800–900 were declared foreigners by the FTs and the rest were convicted foreigners who had declared themselves as foreigners but had travelled without documents. Besides Bangladesh, there are also convicted foreigners from Afghanistan, Myanmar, Pakistan, etc. in Assam jails. As per Mander's report, the number of detainees declared as foreigners by FTs has increased since 2016.

In June 2018, the Union home ministry sanctioned the plea of the Assam government to set up a full-fledged detention centre which could house at least 3,000 persons. The aim was to

---

[8] The interview with Tarun Gogoi was recorded on 5 November 2018.

house those declared foreigners away from regular convicts. In 2017, about 20 bighas of land were sanctioned for it in the Matia area of Goalpara. News reports said the Union home ministry had agreed to sanction ₹47 crore for the purpose. Coming at the time when the final draft of NRC was published in the state, it triggered speculation in the media about the proposed centre's link to the updating process. This, in turn, led to arouse considerable fear among those whose names didn't figure in the final draft, particularly among the poor. There was a spurt in suicides, both among Hindus and Muslims of East Bengal origin, and some from the Koch Rajbonshi community too. Their families told local media that they took their life because they feared possible detention.

9

VOICES FROM DETENTION

IS THERE ANY HOPE?

AMRITA PAUL

Introduction

The Rohingyas form an ethnic group, a majority of whom are Muslims, in the Northern Province of Myanmar (erstwhile Burma), in the State of Rakhine (*Arakan*). They were rendered stateless after the enactment of a new citizenship law in 1982. Continued state-sponsored violence and massacres, now widely regarded as ethnic cleansing, and perpetration of crimes against humanity resulted in a large number of Rohingyas fleeing to other countries for refuge.

August 2017 witnessed the largest migrations of this community when the brutality of State action and suppression by the security forces of Myanmar caused more than 723,000 Rohingya to seek refuge in neighbouring countries – mostly Bangladesh as well as onward movement to India. While the vast majority of the Rohingyas who fled Myanmar are in Bangladesh in refugee camps, approximately 18,000 Rohingya asylum seekers and refugees registered with the United Nations High Commissioner for Refugees (UNHCR) are living in India. Currently, more than a hundred Rohingyas continue to be detained in prisons in the states of West Bengal, Assam and Manipur.

From when the recent crisis first broke out in late 2017 till date, Bangladesh has struggled to deal with the human rights crisis; India, the South Asian power, has issued an advisory to take active steps to identify the ones already in its territory in order to formulate plans for forcible repatriation, thwarting attempts at entry and thereby denying them protection. The matter continues to remain sub-judice in the apex court. Meanwhile, the State practice and international protection norms, i.e. non-refoulment, continue to have a binding value.

The chapter traces the CHRI's journey of involvement and engagement with the authorities while advocating for enhanced documentation and extending available protection models for these refugees caught in detention. Typically, refugees and asylum seekers face long overstays after completing their sentences, without being extended any protection. The attitude of the authorities indicates that in the absence of political will to protect refugees and asylum seekers, the refugees may experience torture and, in the worst cases, death in detention.

A news report in the *New York Times* on 11 January 1982 carried the headline: 'Thai Pirates continuing brutal attacks on Vietnamese Boat People.' It opened with an account of a survivor:

> Nguyen Tien Hoa says he escaped from Vietnam in mid-November aboard a 50-foot boat that carried about 75 refugees, more than half of them women and children. By the end of the month, Mr Hoa, 31 years old, wounded, distraught and alone in a disabled vessel with his 10-year-old brother, drifted ashore in Malaysia, where the boy died of shock and untended injuries.[1]

[1] Barbara Crossette, 'Thai Pirates Continuing Brutal Attacks on Vietnamese Boat People', *New York Times*, 11 January 1982 https://www.nytimes.com/1982/01/11/world/thai-pirates-continuing-brutal-attacks-on-vietnamese-boat-people.html.

Three decades later, on 17 May 2015, the *Guardian* carried a report on Burma's boatpeople who 'faced choice of annihilation or risking their lives at sea'.[2] The report went on to say that, 'They were carried or staggered ashore, some paralysed by malnutrition, others little more than walking skeletons, burnt and dazed from weeks at sea on boats the UN has called "floating coffins".' Above are true incidents separated by more than three decades!

The world woke up twice to read about the 'boat people'; first in the late 1970s and early 1980s when the Vietnamese were fleeing their country by sea following the collapse of the South Vietnamese government in 1975.[3] The second, much closer to memory, was in May 2015, when we read incidents of boats carrying Rohingyas capsized at sea, resulting in deaths. This finally captured the imagination of the 'civilized nations'.[4] Accounts of survivors clarified the *raison d'être* of their presence on those boats. Some hoped to flee continued persecution in Burma only to land up in the hands of smugglers and traffickers, which meant they had to endure months at sea, packed below decks in cramped conditions with limited food, water and poor sanitation. They recounted the horrific treatment that they underwent at the hands of unscrupulous smugglers and traffickers in Burma, coupled with abuse and neglect aboard

---

[2] Emma Graham-Harrison, 'Burma's boatpeople faced choice of annihilation or risking their lives at sea', *The Guardian*, 17 May 2015 https://www.theguardian.com/world/2015/may/17/Rohingya-burma-refugees-boat-migrants.

[3] Lizzie Dearden, 'How Britain treated refugees in the 1980s – one grateful man's story', *Independent*, 9 September 2015 https://www.independent.co.uk/news/uk/home-news/refugee-crisis-son-of-vietnamese-boat-people-shares-story-of-how-britain-treated-asylum-seekers-in-10493316.html.

[4] Sydney Jonathan Pearlman, 'Who are the Rohingya boat people?' *The Telegraph*, 13 February 2020. https://www.telegraph.co.uk/news/worldnews/asia/burmamyanmar/11620933/Who-are-the-Rohingya-boat-people.html.

ships. The year has changed, but Rohingyas continue to flee on boats; boats still capsize and lives are still being lost.[5]

Background

The first large-scale riots between Muslims (Rohingyas) and Buddhists – in Rakhine (erstwhile known as Arakan) state took place in March 1942.[6] During the military rule of Burmese Army General Ne Win, between 1966 and 1988, they continued to face oppression. In 1978, a census (namely *Nagamin* or Dragon King) was undertaken to supposedly clear out illegal immigrants. The Rohingyas experienced brutal violence during this phase along with the destruction of mosques and other Islamic monuments. Murder and mayhem ruled the streets and also contributed to the exodus of more than 200,000 to Bangladesh.[7] Crackdowns continued, and they were forced to flee to other Southeast Asian nations. The final nail in the coffin came with the new citizenship law in 1982, which completely excluded them and eventually made them stateless.[8]

Antagonism towards the Rohingyas originated from a deeply rooted Buddhist nationalism and accumulated sentiments of disbelief, hatred and the fear of the 'other'.[9] The UN Office

---

[5] 'At least 14 dead as Rohingya boat sinks in Bangladesh', *BBC*, 11 February 2020 https://www.bbc.com/news/world-asia-51454107.

[6] Egreteau Renaud, Burma (Myanmar), Online Encyclopaedia of Mass Violence, 19 October 2009, 1930–2007 http://bo-k2s.sciences-po.fr/mass-violence-war-massacre-resistance/en/document/burma-myanmar-1930-2007, ISSN 1961-9898.

[7] Carl Grundy-Warr & Elaine Wong, 'Sanctuary under a plastic sheet: the unresolved problem of Rohingya refugees', 1997, *IBRU Boundary and Security Bulletin*, Autumn, pp. 79–91.

[8] Ahsraful Azad and Fareha Jasmine, 'Durable solutions to the protracted refugee situation: The case of Rohingyas in Bangladesh', *Journal of Indian Research*, Vol. 1, No. 4, 2013, pp. 25–35.

[9] Moshe Yegar, *The Muslims of Burma: A Study of a Minority Group*, Germany: Otto Harrassowitz, Wiesbaden, 1972, pp. 95–106.

for the Coordination of Humanitarian Affairs reported that more than 143,500 remain internally displaced in Rakhine as of August 2015.[10] Many have abandoned their homes and homeland to live in camps in Sittwe (Myanmar) or in other neighbouring countries.

In recent times, the violence against the Rohingyas is chiefly perpetrated by the border police (*Na Sa Ka*[11]). The forms of violence faced by Rohingyas in detention, according to reports, can be grouped under the following:

- *Forced labour:*[12] Most men were routinely picked up to work without any wages. They were beaten mercilessly in addition to inflicting other forms of torture. Digging ponds, carrying loads upon the hill and other work requiring manual labour are imposed upon them. The demand for forced labour from the authorities places a large burden on the Rohingya population as it leaves them with not enough time to do their own work. The frequency of forced labour differs from place to place and from family to family. Protesters usually meet death.
- *Restrictions on movement:*[13] The Rohingyas are virtually confined to their own village tracts. They have to apply for permission to leave, even if it is just to go a nearby village.

---

[10] UNOCHA. 'Myanmar: Internal Displacement in Rakhine State', 2015 http://reliefweb.int/sites/reliefweb.int/files/resources/Affected_Map_IDP_Sites_Rakhine_OCHA_Aug2015_A4.pdf.

[11] Nay-Sat Kut-kwey ye (NaSaKa), a security force consisting of police, military, intelligence, customs officers and riot police, operated in Rakhine State until 2013 under the control of the Ministry for Border Affairs; See also, Andrew Selth, 'Myanmar's Police Forces: Coercion, Continuity and Change' (2012) *Contemporary Southeast Asia*, 34 (1) 53–79.

[12] 'Myanmar's Muslims: The Oppressed of the Oppressed' by Rianne ten Veen, ISBN 1-903718-35-X, Islamic Human Rights Commission, London.

[13] Human Rights Watch (HRW), 'Southeast Asia: Accounts from Rohingya Boat People,' 27 May 2015 https://www.hrw.org/news/2015/05/27/southeast-asia- accounts-Rohingya-boat-people.

Sometimes they have to pay for this permit too. There is no permission for staying out at night as they have to return home by 10 p.m. If anyone is found to cross that time period, they are immediately arrested by the *Na Sa Ka*.

- *Restriction in religious activities:* Mosques were burnt down and during the holy month, the Buddhists would lock up the remaining few mosques. Muslims are forcibly prevented from practising their religion and there have been incidents where they have even been murdered.
- *Restriction on marriage:*[14] Since 1992, a licence was required to enter into a marriage. Restrictions have been stepped up over the years by denying licences, with a view to curb the growth of population. The elders of the couple have to pay arbitrary denominations of money to get a license issued or *latugom* before a marriage ceremony can be held. The amount that they have to pay varies from place to place, family to family. If the girl is good-looking, the fee would be higher.
- *Restriction on children:* Rules have been imposed on the number of children a couple may have i.e. two kids. Non-compliance results in heavy punishment (including imprisonment). Moreover, for the birth registration, a family has to pay 7,000 to 8,000 Kyat. They are even forced to pay tax if their cows give birth to calves.

Many waves of terror and consequent displacement have plagued the community, particularly in the last decade. To escape the continued persecution, they have had to rely on unscrupulous smugglers[15] to 'perceived safety' via sea to southern Thailand

---

[14] A. Lindblom, E. Marsh, T. Motala, and K. Munyan, 'Persecution of the Rohingya Muslims: Is Genocide Occurring in Myanmar's Rakhine State?', 2015 https://www.Fortifyrights.Org/Downloads/Yale_Persecution_Of_The_Rohingya_October_2015.Pdf.

[15] 'Confine Rohingya Refugees To Designated Camps, Record Biometric

or through jungle pathways across the border into northern Malaysia.[16] Many to the tune of 250,000 Rohingya have crossed into Bangladesh, while another 15,000 ultimately made their way to Malaysia.[17]

As for their migration towards Bangladesh, the prima facie recognition was closed with a registration cut-off date in mid-1992. The Rohingyas arrived or returned after the cut-off date were not able to receive the status of refugees and consequently not permitted in the camps.[18] About 30,000 registered Rohingyas, supported by the UN High Commissioner for Refugees (UNHCR), continue to live in Bangladesh around the Cox's Bazar area.

There have been many spurts of violence in the region. Before August 2017, violence escalated in June 2012. On 12 July of 2012,[19] President Thein Sein called for 'illegal' Rohingya to be sent to 'any third country'. The UNHCR

Details: Centre To States', *Daily Star*, 2018, https://m.dailyhunt.in/news/india/english/news+world-epaper-newswore/confine+Rohingya+refugees+to+designated+camps+record+biometric+details+centre+to+states-newsid-89304003; See also Man Aman Singh Chhina, 'Rohingya refugees in Dera Bassi, Lalru areas come under security scanner', *Indian Express*, 20 September 2017 https://indianexpress.com/article/chandigarh/Rohingya-refugees-in-dera-bassi-lalru-areas-come-under-security-scanner-4851856/.

[16] John Roberts, 'Rohingya refugees abused and killed in camps in Malaysia/Thailand', WSWS, 29 May 2015 https://www.wsws.org/en/articles/2015/05/29/refu-m29.html.

[17] Samuel Cheung, 'Migration Control and the Solutions Impasse in South and South East Asia: Implications from the Rohingya Experience', *Journal of Refugee Studies*, Vol. 25, No. 1, March 2012, pp. 50–70.

[18] Jayanta Gupta, 'Khalid's arrest sparks off debate on Rohingyas in India', *Times of India*, 20 November 2014 http://timesofindia.indiatimes.com/india/Khalids-arrest-sparks-off-debate-on-Rohingyas-in-India/articleshow/45220794.cms.

[19] 'Myanmar moots camps or deportation for Rohingyas' *Bangkok Post* Public Company Limited, 12 July 2012 https://www.bangkokpost.com/world/302138/myanmar-moots-camps-or-deportation-for-Rohingyas.

had promptly rejected the proposed plan.[20] Though the government claimed that it had taken the necessary measures to prevent the recurring violence, conflict broke out once again on 21 October 2017.[21]

Looming death has forced the Rohingyas to flee to Bangladesh to find safety and security. Among them, many have charted pathways traversing the heartland of Bangladesh to reach the eastern fringes of the state of West Bengal in search of life and liberty. This migration has not gone unnoticed and has caused many to note serious concerns. A senior intelligence official told *The Hindu* that 'more than one thousand Rohingya refugees had been detained and sent to prisons in the State in the last six months. But the West Bengal government has no clear idea of the actual number of the undocumented immigrants who entered the State in the past few years.'[22] Over the past five years, West Bengal Correctional Homes have housed more than a hundred Rohingyas in detention. Many have been caught by the border security forces and handed over to the police, some at the railway and bus stations inside the territory of India and, in one case, the refugees were arrested when they came to meet their relative in prison.

The CHRI's engagement with this issue begins with the account of Rafia Begum – a Rohingya woman whom we stumbled across in prison. Engaging with her case made us

---

[20] 'UN refugee chief rejects call to resettle Rohingya', *San Diego Union-Tribune*, 12 July 2012 https://www.sandiegouniontribune.com/sdut-un-refugee-chief-rejects-call-to-resettle-Rohingya-2012jul12-story.html.

[21] Dean Nelson, 'Burma considers citizenship for Rohingya Muslims', *The Telegraph*, 1 November 2012 https://www.telegraph.co.uk/news/worldnews/asia/burmamyanmar/9648329/Burma-considers-citizenship-for-Rohingya-Muslims.html.

[22] Suvojit Bagchi, 'Rohingya influx – a brewing crisis', *The Hindu*, 17 March 2014 http://www.thehindu.com/news/national/other-states/Rohingya-influx-a-brewingcrisis/article5797314.ece.

realize that there was a need for examining the larger issue of Rohingya Prisoners.

Detention as a Means of Immigration Control

The CHRI, through its demonstration project,[23] aimed at creating legal awareness among the prisoners – undertrial and convicts – regarding their rights as prisoners during incarceration. Typically, the project, through its clinic, dealt with queries about seeking legal advice and opinion, seeking the assistance in appointment of a legal aid lawyer as well as information regarding the current status of their cases. Among the many who accessed this clinic, at one of the most populous Central Correctional Facility (hereinafter referred to as prison), one woman came with a single query: Would she ever be reunited with her children and family who were residing in Jammu?

Little did we know at the juncture that she was a refugee, who was imprisoned and punished, had served her sentence three years ago but had remained imprisoned because she was a Rohingya; incarcerated as the law was silent on her road to release.

First Tryst with the Rohingya: Rafia Begum

Rafia,[24] a thirty-two-year-old Rohingya woman, had witnessed her home and hearth on fire and mired in blood. After escaping Burma (now Myanmar) along with her seven children, she travelled through Bangladesh and entered India, but was arrested after being apprehended by the border security force. She and

---

[23] Before mandating the setting up of Prison Legal Aid Clinics, CHRI had established along with NUJS students to familiarize the inmates as to their rights at arrest, through their trial as well as educate them on their right to appeal. The project was aimed at creating legal awareness as well as waking up the legal aid framework for the persons in custody.

[24] The name has been changed to protect anonymity.

her children were handed over to the nearest police station where they were arrested and charged under Section 14A(b)[25] of the Foreigner's Act, 1946, in 2009. She was thrown into judicial custody and her children housed in a home under the Juvenile Justice Act. Her 'crime' was that she had entered India without any valid documents to escape persecution at home. She was sentenced to a year of imprisonment and ordered to be repatriated.

Even though her term ended on 1 October 2010, she continued to languish in prison because she was resisting repatriation as she had family in India (Jammu). Also, the conditions were not safe for her to be repatriated to Myanmar. Additionally, to initiate repatriation, the nationality verification step is a prerequisite, which was dependent upon the legal status in the country of origin. She approached the prison legal aid clinic in February 2013 for assistance to gain liberty. The clinic had not come across such a request and, therefore, the first step was to ensure that her case was referred to the UNHCR. To be able to extend protection as well as confirm the refugee status, her details had to be mandatorily registered, followed by a determination process of the claim of being a refugee and thus seeking protection. The catch lay in her being in detention and not at liberty to approach the UNHCR!

---

[25] Penalty for entry in restricted areas, etc. Whoever (b) enters into or stays in any area in India without the valid documents required for such entry or for such stay, as the case may be, under the provisions of any order made under this Act or any direction given in pursuance thereof, shall be punished with imprisonment for a term which shall not be less than two years, but may extend to eight years and shall also be liable to fine which shall not be less than ten thousand rupees but may extend to fifty thousand rupees; and if he has entered into a bond in pursuance of clause (f) of Sub-section (2) of Section 3, his bond shall be forfeited, and any person bound thereby shall pay the penalty thereof, or show cause to the satisfaction of the convicting court why such penalty should not be paid by him.

On 12 December 2013, the Calcutta HC passed an order[26] directing her transfer to Tihar Jail within four weeks. This would facilitate her meeting with her family as well as approaching the UNHCR for the grant of refugee status. Tihar did not respond for four months. On 13 March 2014, the Tihar Jail informed that Rafia was a released prisoner, and she couldn't be confined as it was against the mandate of the Prisons Act, 1894. They suggested that she could be transferred to a detention centre alternatively.

The response received from Tihar necessitated the modification of the order of the Calcutta High Court. On 7 May 2014, the court heard and asked the home department to ascertain the vacancy at the Lampur Detention Centre so that the process was not rendered futile again.

Persistent efforts to confirm the vacancy at the detention centre informed that it was only for housing male prisoners. As for female prisoners, the government of Delhi had many homes which would have to be utilized. This highlighted the absence of protocols and information available to carve out solutions for exceptionally vulnerable instances.

The CHRI contacted the Mahila Sadan in the Nirmal Chhaya complex to persuade them to take in Rafia at one of their homes. Due to the exceptionality of the case, they agreed to extend their cooperation and house her at one of the short-stay homes. After a delay of two months, on 3 July 2014,[27] the court recognized the plight of Rafia Begum and ordered her transfer to Mahila Sadan, Nirmal Chhaya Complex. She was transferred to Delhi on 19 July 2014. But the next leg of the battle was still to be won.

---

[26] Johra Begum, *Jahiri Bibi vs the Union of India & Ors.* W.P. 14050 OF 2014 & WP 33910 OF 2013. Available: https://www.humanrightsinitiative.org/download/1456994348Johra%20Begum%20vs.%20Union%20of%20India.pdf.

[27] Ibid.

For the grant of her refugee status, it took less than half a year to conduct the determination interview and confirm the status. The UNHCR noted that her long confinement past her completion of sentence coupled with isolation had affected her mental stability greatly even though her protection claim was genuine.

Even though this case witnessed many agencies synergizing and concurring the special nature of the case, the systemic failures and barriers brought to light the absence of a policy to handle such cases in the future. It proved that the process of churning showcases more disappointment and the search for liberty is elusive. It was the relentless effort of the family and human rights defenders which enabled her release from behind bars. This intervention also made clear the need to identify such persons in detention who are refugees/asylum seekers and need the protection of the UNHCR.

Toil for Documentation

Rafia's case emphasized the need of documentation, especially of the refugees and asylum seekers in detention. One of the key reasons to facilitate documentation was to acknowledge the figures/number of refugees in detention in the correctional facilities of West Bengal. Apart from identifying them among the masses in prisons, it would also inform the prison functionaries about the difference in legal status. The process of documentation was implemented with active help and assistance from the staff at respective prisons. For this, dialogue and advocacy[28] was built

[28] *Guide for Prison Officers: Refugees & Asylum Seekers*. Available: https://www.humanrightsinitiative.org/download/1528281092Guide%20for%20Prison%20Officers%20Refugees%20&%20Asylum%20Seekers.pdf; *A Basic Guide: Defending Asylum Seekers in Detention*. Available: https://www.humanrightsinitiative.org/download/1523869385A%20Basic%20guidebook%20-%20Defending%20Asylum%20Seekers%20in%20Detention.pdf.

to educate and inform the first contact at these prisons for them to be cautious and know the perils of the life of a Rohingya in their villages, the reasons for their flight and the legal protection they are owed by the international community to uphold human rights tenets. Basic information of the refugees in detention detailed the reasons of flight, information on family members outside – Burma, Bangladesh and India – and in detention and the travel history – tracing the ways and means of reaching Bangladesh, traversing the country and entering India (including the reason for the same). Among the many exchanges, a few always evoke sympathy.

> '... I ran from my house to the hills and never looked back ... I was scared that I was followed and may meet the same end as my brother. I can still hear my mother say run and don't look back ...' – Nur Mohammed

> '... I saw the army (*na sa ka*) slaughter (*harahari*) my parents from the gap of the door in the barn of my house. I can't sleep; I keep seeing them in my dreams. I ran to my uncle's place and joined them when they ran away ...' – Shah Alam

Each of them has countless experiences of grave persecution they have lived through in their homeland. While collecting the basic information from each individual, developing a format for capturing these pieces of responses was found to be essential. This could serve as the stepping stone to the registration which is conducted at the Delhi office of the UNHCR. This resulted in developing the 'in-absentia registration form'[29].

As the name suggests, this would be employed for persons in custody/confinement to aid in their registration. The registration

[29] In-Absentia Registration Form. Available: https://humanrightsinitiative.org/download/Basic%20Registration%20Form%20for%20detention%20cases.pdf.

details would be the basis for generating an interview date for which permissions would have to be sought to conduct the Refugee Status Determination (RSD) process in detention. The new format has been utilized for initiating registration for the Rohingyas in detention and informing the UNHCR every time a refugee is found behind bars and in want of assistance. The format would also help in populating information about their case status and prisoner category in the prison.

'Protected in Peril': The Case Study of *Md. Nasir & Ors*[30]

Interventions and engagement to strive towards initiating release of Rohingyas from detention have met with success in the past.[31] Md. Nasir and five others had travelled to Murshidabad (one of the districts of West Bengal) to meet another Rohingya in detention at the Central Correctional Home. But in contravention of their protection vis-à-vis the 'refugee' status granted by the UNHCR, they were arrested by the police from the Berhampore Barrack Square Ground. As regards their refugee cards, neither were they admitted in court nor mentioned in the seizure list and there was a high probability of them being destroyed.

During the process of documentation of the Rohingyas in detention, the CHRI was informed about the case. The CHRI coordinated with the legal aid lawyer towards the release of the five Rohingyas in detention. Adequate support was extended through documentation, such as evidence as to their persecution in their country of origin to the legal aid lawyer, who was able to convince the judicial officer regarding the human rights violations they had suffered and their legal status in India through the UNHCR. The process required the verification of

---

[30] Name changed to protect anonymity.

[31] 'Five Rohingya Refugees freed from Indian Jail' *Asia News*, 4 June 2016 http://www.asianews.network/content/five-Rohingya-refugees-freed-indian-jail-18738.

the 'status' as ordered by the court and, thereafter, successful defence placed on record to prove the same.

The case highlighted and brought to the fore the concern about the absence of knowledge among the police and border security forces vis-à-vis the refugee protection standards as secured through the mandate of the UNHCR. Furthermore, this prompted efforts to seek permissions and undertake the Refugee Status Determination (RSD) process for the refugees in detention to secure protection for them.

Due to the positive decisions in the subordinate judiciary, the RSD missions were planned and executed in the Correctional Homes housing them across the state of West Bengal. Utilizing the previous orders' implementation, the persuasive value of the practice may prevail in other courts where similar orders may be sought. The hope was to conduct the determination interviews, process the claims at the end of the UNHCR and issue refugee cards which would be pleaded towards discharge of cases instituted against them under the Foreigners Act, 1946.

According to international law, there exists a distinction between who is a foreigner and a refugee. Broadly speaking, there are two well-defined groups of foreigners, different from that of a 'refugee'. These are:

- *Temporary residents, tourists and travellers:* People in this category come to India for a specific purpose and duration with the prior permission (visa) of the government. Certain conditions may arise during the stay, which may endanger their lives and liberty due to which they request protection. Each case is dealt with according to merits and circumstances.
- *Illegal economic migrants:* These persons have left their country of origin without authorization and entered a destination country without legal permission only in the pursuit of being economically sound. They are not refugees, but illegal migrants and would be dealt with accordingly under the Foreigners Act, Indian Passport Act, Criminal Acts etc.

As for the treatment of foreigners in detention, international law is emboldened and succinct due to the existence of standards and obligations owed under globally accepted conventions.

On the other hand, a person becomes a refugee because of circumstances which are beyond that person's control, often distressing. The person is fleeing due to criminal discrimination and persecution due to socioeconomic and political insecurity, generalized violence, civil war or ethnic strife – all of which lead to a well-founded fear of it continuing. (Refugee Convention, 1951 – Definition clause).

As regards the legal implication in the Indian context, there is no separate legal instrument to treat and respond to the human rights violations suffered by them. Due to the absence of a legal framework, the response to individuals fleeing across the border is met with apprehension and followed by detention.

Confinement in the Name of Care: The Case Study of Yasmin

In March 2016, Yasmin,[32] aged fourteen, having fled from Myanmar (via Bangladesh), accompanied her father and uncle in escaping the excesses of the military and entered India. The group was apprehended at the border and handed over to the nearest police station and, thereafter, charged under the Foreigners Act. In view of her juvenility, she was ordered by the Juvenile Board to be housed at a shelter home, while her father was incarcerated in the state correctional facility. Her mother and brother were living in Hyderabad at the time.

In the practice of the child rights framework, the principle of the best interests of the child[33] is of crucial nature and has

---

[32] Name changed to protect anonymity.

[33] E. D. Pask, 'Unaccompanied Refugee and Displaced Children: Jurisdiction, Decision-Making and Representation', *International Journal of Refugee Law 199*, Vol. 1, No. 2, 1989, p. 201, citing *Children Deprived of a Normal Home Life*, E/CN.5/271, 1952, pp. 7–8 as cited in J. M. Pobjoy, *The*

been the subject of extensive consideration in academic and operational circles. Nonetheless, no such assessment was carried out by any competent authority. Usually abbreviated as BIA, the best interests assessment is designed to ensure that the child's best interests are given utmost importance. The CHRI received information from the father incarcerated in the correctional home to restore the minor to the family. Permissions were sought from the authorities of the home to interview the juvenile and conduct the BIA. The assessment was duly recorded and shared with the UNHCR to process the requisite documentation, which would facilitate protection and liberty from the home as well as restoration to the family.

The CHRI, along with the lawyer from Human Rights Law Network (HRLN), represented the case before the Juvenile Justice Board and convinced them that the minor was not in conflict with the law (CCL) but rather a child in need of care and protection (CNCP) in light of the motivations of the migration from Myanmar to India. Yasmin's mother and brother, residing in Hyderabad, were convinced to travel to Kolkata to take custody of her. After the board was convinced of her need for protection, the matter was referred to the Child Welfare Committee (CWC) as envisaged under the Juvenile Justice Act, 2005. The committee passed the requisite order restoring and reuniting the family unit after seventeen months.

This was one such case where the CHRI intervened and met with success. Children continue to be 'detained' either while accompanying their parents or even unaccompanied; but efforts are taken to realize the motivation of the migration and thereby affect the status during the inquiry where they are mistaken as children in conflict with law (CCL), rather than children in

---

Child in International Refugee Law, Cambridge: Cambridge University Press, 2016, p. 203. Also, Preamble of the Juvenile Justice (Care & Protection of Children) Act, 2015, in the Indian context.

need of care and protection (CNCP). Due to the unique status of these children, efforts must be undertaken by authorities to not indiscriminately confine them and restore them to their parents and/or relatives (after satisfaction). Sensitization of the officials of relevant authorities with respect to protection models for these children is paramount.

Break in the Glass

August 2017 saw the release of an advisory from the Ministry of Home Affairs titled 'Identification of Illegal Migrants and Monitoring Thereof'.[34] The contents and intention of this document ran counter to the Constitution of India and international commitments. The advisory specifically empowers the police to detect, arrest and deport the Rohingyas to prevent 'an untoward incident'. India is a state party to both Article 6 and 7 of the International Covenant on Civil and Political Rights (ICCPR), which upholds the right to life and right against inhuman or degrading treatment or punishment.

The deportation of Rohingya Muslims back to Myanmar would be violation of both the above-mentioned provisions of the convention as it prohibits 'to extradite, deport, expel or otherwise remove a person from their territory, where there are substantial grounds for believing that there is a real risk of irreparable harm'. Forcible return of asylum seekers and refugees would violate the customary international law principle of *non-refoulement* – which is binding on India – that forbids states from forcibly returning people to a country where they would be at real risk of serious human rights violations. There is enough literature and evidence to suggest the same.[35]

---

[34] MHA Advisory on Identification of Illegal Migrants and monitoring thereof, 8 August 2017. Available: https://mha.gov.in/sites/default/files/advisoryonillegalmigrant_10092017_2.PDF.

[35] 'Rohingya refugee crisis a "human rights nightmare," UN chief

The advisory has been challenged[36] by two Rohingya immigrants – Mohammad Salimullah and Mohammad Shaqir – on the basis of it being contrary to constitutional protections of Article 14 (Right to equality), Article 21 (Right to life) and Article 51(c), as these are equal rights and liberty accruable to all persons. Of the many pitfalls of the advisory, the most marked was the one which resulted in no favourable orders from judiciary to acknowledge the status of Rohingyas detained in prisons/correctional facilities. This also marked a period of lull where status quo was maintained with respect to the adjudication of these cases and, ultimately, caused longer periods of incarceration with no clear mechanisms of attaining liberty.

Expanding the Canvas of Interest: The Northeast

Caught between Buddhist-dominated Myanmar and Muslim-dominated Bangladesh, recent changes in the policies have prompted the Rohingyas to enter India through the Northeast.[37] There, they are vulnerable to exploitation[38] due to their lack

---

tells Security Council' https://news.un.org/en/story/2017/09/567402-Rohingya-refugee-crisis-human-rights-nightmare-un-chief-tells-security-council; References made in the Kofi Annan Report [Towards a Peaceful, Fair and Prosperous Future for the People of Rakhine: Final Report of the Advisory Commission on Rakhine State, August 2017. Available: http://www.rakhinecommission.org/app/uploads/2017/08/FinalReport_Eng.pdf.

[36] 'SC to hear plea against deportation of Rohingyas', *Indian Express*, 2 September 2017 https://indianexpress.com/article/india/sc-to-hear-plea-against-deportation-of-Rohingyas-4824598/.

[37] 'Nine Rohingyas arrested in Manipur', *Deccan Herald*, 1 June 2019 https://www.deccanherald.com/national/nine-Rohingyas-arrested-in-manipur-737563.html; Debraj Deb, 'Tripura: No consensus on Rohingyas stuck between India-Bangladesh border', *Indian Express*, 21 January 2019 https://indianexpress.com/article/north-east-india/tripura/tripura-stranded-Rohingya-refugees-india-bangladesh-borders-5548896/.

[38] Annie Banerji, 'Indian Police rescue suspected Rohingya victims of trafficking', Reuters, 6 May 2019 https://www.reuters.com/article/

of official identification documents, their inability to speak local languages and their lack of financial means. They have often reported that there is a growing fear of being detained by the Indian border security forces while trying to cross from Bangladesh to India. Several of them experienced shortage of food or water during their journeys. With the grip tightening on the western border of Bangladesh, the route has undergone changes with attempts to enter the states of Assam, Manipur, Tripura and Mizoram. Resultantly, the numbers of Rohingya detainees in prisons and childcare institutions of the North-eastern states have seen an upward trend.

Changes in the demography of the prisons in these states and the absence of capacity on part of the system to respond, prompted the CHRI to seek requisite permissions to access and create legal awareness among the stakeholders, comprising prison administration, legal aid functionaries in addition to the detainees. Utilizing the learnings from the West Bengal experience, documentation and consequent Under Consideration Certificate (UCC) were processed at the earliest. These were shared with the authorities – prison and legal aid – as well as the detainees.

Among the states under consideration, instances of being released on bail are limited to Manipur. Lower courts seemed promising as the trend to release some on bail with conditions i.e. submitting cash as well as committing sureties has been recorded and welcomed.

Both the states of Manipur and Tripura have witnessed minor Rohingyas being housed in shelter homes for care and protection but are very cognizant of the nature and reason of flight. Delays in requisite steps taken in their cases were highlighted, which has been acted upon by the relevant authority. Instances of

---

us-india-Rohingya-trafficking/indian-police-rescue-suspected-Rohingya-victims-of-trafficking-idUSKCN1SC1HO.

restoration to the family have also been noted in Manipur where the proactive role of the lawyer has resulted in their release and return to home subsequently.

Support has also been extended in the form of financial outlays and physical handover when it came to the implementation of the order of a Child Welfare Committee in Tripura. Even though the directions had been passed to restore the minors to the family in Delhi, the administration was unable to implement the same. A rights-based organization extended their support to assist the department in facilitating the transfer to Delhi for ultimate restoration.

Assam has also reported its share of refugees in detention. Many have had to undergo long years of wait in incarceration as articulation of their rights has escaped both merit and responsible adjudication. On the contrary, 2018 and 2019 have witnessed 'consensual' returns being effectuated from the prisons of the state of Assam via the Moreh border in Manipur.[39]

Disguising Consent for Return

The long years of wait behind bars forced many to lose patience and opt for consenting to return to Myanmar. Fearing more years spent far from homeland and an added fear of repatriation in light of the advisory, a few of them consented to return home to their pillaged villages. Md Shamsher Ali was one among them. When reminded of the atrocities reported over the last ten years,

---

[39] Zahir Hussain, 'India deports second Rohingya group to Myanmar, more expulsions likely', Reuters, 3 January 2019 https://www.reuters.com/article/us-myanmar-Rohingya-india/india-deports-second-Rohingya-group-to-myanmar-more-expulsions-likely-idUSKCN1OX0FE; Geeta Mohan, 'Row as government sends 7 Rohingya immigrants back to Myanmar', *India Today*, 5 October 2018 https://www.indiatoday.in/mail-today/story/row-as-government-sends-7-Rohingya-immigrants-back-to-myanmar-1356092-2018-10-05.

he reminded of the same length of time spent in Indian prison. Though he had never been ostracized or made to sleep without food in his stomach, he saw his two children grow up behind bars. He hopes to reach his village to find his parents alive. And if death knocks at his door, he would at least die at home and not be buried in an unmarked grave.

Consent in these circumstances begs to be evaluated and revisited. A straitjacket formula may not be applicable to assess whether the return was undeniably voluntary or not. The legal framework holds that in instances of voluntary return, the person loses the protection that was governing his personality. But the practicality of all systems at play creates that window where the meaning of consent in voluntary return needs further dialogue.

The Way Forward: '*Durability*' of Durable Solutions or Context-Specific Solution

India is not a signatory to the UN Convention Relating to the Status of Refugees, 1951, and its Protocol Relating to the Status of Refugees, 1967[40]; neither does it have a singular domestic refugee policy.[41] On the one hand, Indian policy on the issue of refugee rights has been witnessed in the state practice where in a steady flow of refugees have preferred India as a haven – also complimented by the international commitments through conventions and treaties. The sheer list of acts, rules and

---

[40] UNHCR. Convention and Protocol Relating to the Status of Refugees http://www.unhcr.org/3b66c2aa10.html

[41] India hosts over 200,000 refugees and asylum seekers – Tibetans and Sri Lankan Tamils – and has been lauded for its tradition of accepting refugees. The position became stringent towards Rohingya. See, K. Yhome, *Examining India's stance on the Rohingya crisis*. The Observer Research Foundation, 2018. Available: https://www.orfonline.org/wpcontent/uploads/2018/07/ORF_IssueBrief_247_Rohingya_FinalForUpload.pdf.

guidelines issued at different times poses a significant problem to both the executive and the judiciary in dealing with the refugee issues, as it impacts the implementation of the law.

Even though India has had a tradition of hosting many refugee communities, two major factors appear to have influenced the action of the Indian Government vis-à-vis the according of protection to Rohingyas in India. The first being their Muslim identity.[42] The political climate under the aegis of the present government has witnessed an increase in anti-Muslim sentiment, engulfing the Rohingya crisis.[43] There has been an active portrayal of the Rohingyas as radicals and potential threats to national security[44], even though it has not been proven as of yet. The Citizenship Amendment Act, 2019, has triggered dissent in India and been hailed as discriminatory; for the Rohingyas, it's a tragic fate[45] and no different from their times in Burma. Even in the face of the pandemic, the government issued an advisory[46] opting for 'selective discrimination' on the basis of their faith

---

[42] R. Sriram, 'View: Keep out Rohingyas. India must practice hard state politics', *Economic Times*, 11 September 2017. https://economictimes.indiatimes.com/news/politics-and-nation/view-keep-out-Rohingyas-india-must-practice-hard-state-politics/articleshow/60453325.cms?from=mdr.

[43] Ashley Starr Kinseth, 'India's Rohingya Shame' *Al Jazeera*, 29 January 2019 https://www.aljazeera.com/indepth/opinion/india-Rohingya-shame-190125104433377.html.

[44] Gaurav Vivek Bhatnagar, 'States to Collect Biometric Data of Rohingya to Take Action with Myanmar: Rajnath Singh', *The Wire*, 1 October 2018 https://thewire.in/politics/states-to-collect-biometric-data-of-Rohingya-to-take-action-with-myanmar-rajnath-singh.

[45] 'CAA: Centre's next step will be to deport Rohingya refugees, says Union minister', *Scroll.in*, 3 January 2020. https://scroll.in/latest/948687/caa-centres-next-step-will-be-to-deport-Rohingya-muslims-says-union-minister.

[46] Ananya Bhardwaj, 'Govt wants Rohingya Muslims in India tested after Tablighi Jamaat link emerges', *The Print*, New Delhi, 17 April 2020. https://theprint.in/india/governance/govt-wants-Rohingya-muslims-in-india-tested-after-tablighi-jamaat-link-emerges/404097/

with complete disregard to them battling 'Islamophobia' and hunger.[47]

The other factor is that they are often confused with Bangladeshis, owing to similarities in the language and appearances. The migration of Bangladeshis is on the account of economic reasons and has been brought under the 'rubric of national security'.[48] Migration across the border has been perceived as an affront and much effort has been taken to put in place border controls, determination of nationalities – identification, detention and forcible 'pushback' (deportation in some instances). In our interactions with Rohingyas, they have confirmed that they have often crossed along with Bangladeshi migrants.

On the diplomatic front, the Indian government has clearly not been supportive of the Rohingyas, with India abstaining from voting on the UN Resolution on the Situation of Rohingya Muslims and other Minorities in Myanmar in 2017.[49] India's soft approach is understood to be rooted in security needs and geopolitical compulsions.[50] The above factors and posturing have increased the insecurity felt by the community in India and have also been instrumental in some families leaving the country and others considering to follow suit.[51]

---

[47] Tapan Kumar Bose, 'COVID-19: Rohingya Refugees in India Are Battling Islamophobia and Starvation', *The Wire*, 1 May 2020 https://thewire.in/rights/india-Rohingya-refugees-starvation-covid-19.

[48] Pushpita Das, 'Illegal Migration from Bangladesh – Deportation, Border Fences and Work Permits', IDSA Monograph Series No. 56, 2016, p. 12. Available: https://idsa.in/system/files/monograph/monograph56.pdf.

[49] Resolution 72/248. https://digitallibrary.un.org/record/1470211?ln=en (For the Voting Pattern).

[50] Harsh V. Pant, 'Indias Balancing Act in Myanmar', *The Diplomat*, 9 September 2017 https://thediplomat.com/2017/09/indias-balancing-act-in-myanmar/.

[51] Harsh Nambiar, 'Why leaving Jammu's 10,000 Rohingyas with no

This chapter is focused on the detention experiences and the conditions of Rohingyas in India. Many reasons exist for them to flee. They are attracted to India, which holds a promise of life. As there is a presence of community life and security in India, they too play a part in migration decisions; still the movement of Rohingyas is forced migration.

The migration of the Rohingya is due to the well-documented and planned persecution that they have faced in Burma. The migration will continue till solutions have been engineered to afford them a safe world. In this regard, if we are to assess the applicability of durable solutions, neither voluntary repatriation nor local integration seems to be a way forward. Even though voluntary repatriation has been regarded as the most preferred solution, many factors have to be considered.[52] Broadly, conditions in the home country, safety and security in the form of guarantees and the existence of a legal framework to protect the rights and interests of the returnees in addition to monitoring the return.[53] Instances of prosecuting Rohingya who were attempting to flee have also surfaced[54], which does not encourage vast majorities to return. Torture had been meted out to a few who returned from Bangladesh to collect belongings in

---

choice may be the biggest threat', *The Economic Times*, 24 September 2017. http://economictimes.indiatimes.com/articleshow/60809214.cms?utm_source=contentofinterest&utm_medium=text&utm_campaign=cppst.

[52] G. Goodwin-Gill, 'Voluntary Repatriation: Legal and Policy Issues', Oxford: Clarendon Press, 1989, pp. 255–91.

[53] UN High Commissioner for Refugees (UNHCR), Handbook – *Voluntary Repatriation: International Protection*, January 1996, available at: https://www.refworld.org/docid/3ae6b3510.html.

[54] 'Myanmar Court Jails 15 Rohingya For Two Years For Trying to Flee Country', Radio Free Asia, 6 March 2020 https://www.rfa.org/english/news/myanmar/Rohingya-jailed-03062020155637.html.

Burma.[55] Lastly, when communication has been severed with the outside world,[56] *truth* can be easily masked.

Local integration lacks a formal definition, but Article 34 of the convention affords a skeleton by facilitating assimilation and naturalization of the refugee. This can only be achieved with the agreement of the government of host/asylum country. With the critical move in 2017, which led to drastic changes for the security of the Rohingya in India, this proposition also does not pass muster.

For those who can neither voluntarily return to their country of origin nor safely remain in their country of refuge, the only solution is to resettle in a third country. Some countries accept only a set number of refugees every year as part of their immigration policy; furthermore, this is the least desirable solution, apart from being cumbersome as well as most costly.[57]

In the interim, to express commitment of the international community to respond to large movements of refugees and migrants as well as ease pressure on host countries, the UNGA unanimously adopted the New York Declaration for Refugees and Migrants in 2016. This sets out the Comprehensive Refugee Response Framework (CRRF). Joint Response Plans have also been put together after the International Fact-finding Mission on Myanmar submitted its report.[58]

---

[55] Mark Inkey, 'The Nightmare Awaiting Rohingya Returnees', *The Diplomat*, 19 September 2018 https://thediplomat.com/2018/09/the-nightmare-awaiting-Rohingya-returnees/.

[56] Verena Hölzl, 'Bangladesh's internet crackdown further isolates Rohingya refugees', *The New Humanitarian*, 10 March 2020 https://www.thenewhumanitarian.org/2020/03/10/Rohingya-refugees-internet-ban-bangladesh.

[57] UNHCR, FAQs about Resettlement, September 2013. Available: https://www.refworld.org/pdfid/4ac0d7e52.pdf.

[58] Situation of human rights of Rohingya Muslims and other minorities in Myanmar, A/HRC/39/L.22. Available: https://documents-dds-ny.un.org/doc/UNDOC/LTD/G18/285/92/PDF/G1828592.pdf?OpenElement;

Alternatives to Detention

To deter detention, which has been growing over the last twenty years to control and tighten borders[59], alternatives need to be defined and devised. Detention is being used to address broad social and political issues as well as responding to political pressure.[60] It may be perceived as a symbolic act in addition to its physical and mental impact. There is no denying that complex issues are at play, but it cannot be the preferred solution – detention is not an effective deterrent, it is not useful as a means to case resolution, it has been shown to cause harm to the physical and mental well-being of a person, antithetical to the principles of human rights at its core and, finally, it is expensive for the State.

'Alternatives' for the refugees and asylum seekers would uphold their rights as well as avoid the harms of detention, reduce exposure to overcrowding and long-term detention and enable greater access to programmes that support health and welfare.

Elements of the alternatives must be considered on the parameters of being cost-effective, supporting compliance mechanisms and measuring intangible outcomes. Focusing on devising mechanisms of community placement and screening towards a holistic case resolution and management is advised.

Report of the international independent fact-finding mission on Myanmar submitted the Advance Edited version. Available: https://www.ohchr.org/Documents/HRBodies/HRCouncil/FFM-Myanmar/A_HRC_39_64.pdf.

[59] Amy Nethery and Stephanie J. Silverman, eds. *Immigration Detention: The Migration of a Policy and Its Human Impact* (Ashgate: Routledge, 2015); 'Does Detention Deter?' IDC Briefing Paper, April 2015 (available at https://idcoalition.org/wp-content/uploads/2015/04/Briefing-Paper_Does-Detention-Deter_April-2015-A4_web.pdf)

[60] Arjen Leerkes and Dennis Broeders, 'A Case of Mixed Motives? Formal and Informal Functions of Administrative Immigration Detention,' *British Journal of Criminology* 50, No. 5, 2010: pp. 830–50.

The process must be fair and timely and basic rights and needs must be respected. Opportunities to reside legally and/or voluntary return may also be explored. Coercion and violations must be checked at all times. These practices will limit or erase instances of violations of national laws and to etch out a life in compliance with the norms.

In conclusion, civilized nations need to depart from detention as a means of immigration control to make way for devising alternatives. A recurrent theme running through the conversations with refugees on detention has iterated: 'We will never go to Burma. They will kill us.' This is fast changing due to the advisory in August 2017 and resultant posturing.

Negotiations have been underway for facilitating a return, but the unease lies in the Myanmar government not recognizing the Rohingyas as their citizens and their unwillingness is a point of worry. As demanded by the community, the return has to be on the bedrock of ensuring the protection of the law and guarantees of fundamental rights and freedoms. Premature return may risk the flaring of a volatile circumstance.

In this regard, it may be argued that the instances of the recent returnees should have been avoided. Without a free and fair assessment of the motivations of the returnee (to confirm the absence of force and coercion), the act has been violative of the legal obligation of 'civilized states'. This reduces them to being recipients without having to enforce 'consent' and little role in the aftermath of their actions. In this view, adopting a more coordinated and context-specific approach can help inch towards a lasting solution. This begins with addressing the root causes and reversing those to ensure conditions are created for a safe and secure return voluntarily. There is an urgent need to listen to the voices of refugees and their demands for accountability. Finally, detention as a measure of immigration control in the subcontinent has to be kept aside in order to share the responsibility of upholding human rights standards.[61]

---

[61] The author wishes to thank Palak Choudhury, CHRI, for her valuable comments and inputs at the initial stages of discussion for this essay. This piece took its current shape with her inputs, which are acknowledged deeply. The author is indebted to each Rohingya in detention – to be made part of their lives in retelling their stories of ruthlessness and hot pursuit. This is an attempt to give a window to the hope left in the hearts of those behind bars, who have become stateless and remain far removed from the protection of the host state. At the end, the author hopes that the plight of the Rohingya felt by them echoes through the halls of power and efforts are adopted to secure them human rights by virtue of the fact that they are our fellow human beings on the planet.

10

A STUDY OF THE EDUCATIONAL STATUS OF CHILDREN WITH PARENTS IMPRISONED IN THE SOUTHERN DISTRICTS OF TAMIL NADU

K. R. Raja

Any discussion on prisoners in a sympathetic manner generally evokes a sharp response. Prisoners are generally perceived by the public as dangerous criminals deserving of no mercy. We have noted that every year, more children are separated from parents due to crime than divorce. India is home to almost 19 per cent of the world's children. More than one-third of the country's population, around 440 million, is below the age of eighteen. According to a study, 40 per cent of these children need care and protection, which indicates the magnitude of the problem. In a country like India, with its multicultural, multi-ethnic and multi-religious population, the issues of socially marginalized and economically backward groups are immense. Within such groups, the most vulnerable section is always the children.[1]

[1] Study on Child Abuse, Ministry of Women and Child Development Government of India, 2007.

Invariably, they become the secondary victims of the crime, suffering invisibly due to the imprisonment of their parents.

The challenges lie in reaching out to the most vulnerable, socially excluded children of this country and assessing their educational status. The pressent essay highlights the importance of providing education to the children of prisoners and creating an environment wherein not only is every child protected, but s/he also has access to opportunities and education for her/his all-round growth and development.

Introduction

The primary focus of this study is to identify the children afflicted due to parental imprisonment and crime. Children with imprisoned parents are up to three times more likely to suffer from mental health problems. They are also seven times more likely to commit crime than others.

They become secondary victims of crime, experiencing residential disruptions, school changes, separation from siblings, foster care or periods of time spent with convenient but inappropriate caretakers. They may have witnessed a traumatic scene at the time of the crime and their parents' subsequent arrest. They feel shame, isolation, abandonment, confusion, grief and loneliness. Well-meaning family members encourage keeping the secret from friends and teachers, adding to the sense of stigma, and isolate them from potential supports. Moreover, parents' imprisonment often affects families already challenged by poverty, inadequate housing, abusive or exploitative partners, mental illness, substance abuse and the legacies of child abuse. Even after their parents' returns, children are forever changed simply by knowing they could be gone again.

Need for a Comprehensive Study

Before engulfing ourselves in this onerous task, we want to observe this streak of humanness that a criminal case inherently exhibits in its narration and a close reading of the case documents. The Sessions Judge Mahilar Neethimandram, (Family Court) Thoothukudi, while finding a man guilty under Section 302 of IPC, noted that the accused had come before the court with his three young sons with no one to care for them at home and brought them to court totally unaware and ignorant of what was to take place at the court on that day; therefore, he was seen breaking down continuously in sobs in front of the judge as she was pronouncing the judgment.

Moved by those tears, arising out of a deep anxiety of a father about his three sons who were already deprived of the care of their mother mixed with the fears of uncertainty as to who would look after them while he was in jail undergoing his sentence, the sessions judge immediately referred the three young boys for their care and custody to the Child Welfare Committee of Thoothukudi District. This act of humanness has to be recognized as the basis of appreciation for the learned sessions judge.

Data Collection

In light of the above case, the Hon'ble Madras High Court of Madurai Bench constituted committees which would study every central prison and special prison for women to identify the vulnerabilities of the children of persons in prison and find out measures to be undertaken for those young citizens. The eight teams thus constituted authored a report on the Madurai, Palayamkottai, Trichy, Cuddalore, Salem, Coimbatore, Vellore and Puzhal central prisons. We have utilized those reports as our secondary data to complete our field-level home visits to assess the living conditions of the children with a parent imprisoned in the Palayamkottai and Madurai central prisons. We have also accessed the nominal rolls of each person imprisoned in the above-mentioned central prisons for our reference as secondary data. From a pilot study conducted by the authors during the months of August 2018 to January 2019, we were able to identify the challenges of the children who had a parent imprisoned in the Palayamkottai and Madurai central prisons.

Holistic Consideration of the Needs of the Children

We realized, therefore, not only the enormity of the problems faced by the children with an imprisoned parent, but also that though our mandate was to identify the challenges in reaching out to those children in need of care and protection and propose measures, for the sake of a holistic proposition, we also wanted to expand our mandate and address on an equal footing the children of the victims of violence.

The holistic consideration of attending to the long-term care and protection of the children of victims of the crime and the children of the perpetrators of the crime will thus ensure that our proposals are appreciated in a wholesome manner, and we do not discriminate among children, whether they are denied their humanness and rights as children of victims of the violence or as children with imprisoned parents. There are evidence-based studies which revealed that:

- Children between the ages of 2–6 can feel separation, anxiety, impaired socio-emotional development, traumatic stress and even survivors' guilt.
- Children between the ages of 7–10 may experience developmental regressions, poor self-concept, acute traumatic stress reactions and impaired ability to overcome future trauma.

- Children from ages 11–14 may experience rejection on limits of behaviour and trauma-reactive behaviours.
- Children from the ages of 15–18 may experience a premature termination of dependency relationship with parent, which may lead them to intergenerational crime and incarceration.

Present Living Conditions of the Children with Imprisoned Parents

The total number of convicts in jails in Tamil Nadu was 4,648 as on 31 December 2017. As on 31 January 2019, there are twenty-one inmates in the Palayamkottai and Madurai central prisons serving life terms for cases of spouse murder under sections 302 and 498(a) of the Indian Penal Code. The twenty-one inmates have left a total of forty-eight children without parental care. Out of them, twenty-five are boys and twenty-three girls who have been deprived of all parental care due to crime and imprisonment; in most cases the children are eyewitnesses to the crime. They live with the support of ailing grandparents who aren't able to meet their basic emotional and educational needs due to no income.

The field-level study carried out by travelling extensively, a total of 6,257 kilometres, to reach out to ninety-eight families of prisoners in the Madurai Region and 127 families of prisoners in the Tirunelveli Region. We have identified 177 children in Madurai Region and 254 children in the Tirunelveli Region. For this study, we took samples of 145 families of the prisoners and their 250 children. The families belong to two regions under the jurisdiction of Palayamkottai and Madurai central prisons, comprising seven districts, namely, Madurai, Theni, Dindigul, Sivagangai, Ramanathapuram, Virudhunagar and Thoothukudi. Out of the 250 children, we identified 124 male and 126 female children and assessed their living conditions.

Table 1: Personal Attributes of Survey

Characteristics	*No. of Children*	*Percentage (in %)*
Age (In Years)		
Up to 5	12	4.8
5–10	45	18
10–15	83	33.2
15–18	110	44
Gender		
Male	124	49.6
Female	126	50.4

Most of them don't have access to proper food and other basic amenities such as toilets, regular transportation to go to school. Almost 87 per cent of the children have to spend their vacations in their house as there are no relatives interested in inviting them. There is no regular communication with relatives after their parent is imprisoned. Until they reveal the fact of their parents' imprisonment, there is no conflict with the peer groups at their schools. Once they do, few peers speak to these children. On an average, about twenty children drop out from schools due to abject poverty (Tables 2 and 3).

Table 2: Educational Status of the Children (Class Studying in percentage)

Primary Level	62	24.8
Intermediate Level	51	20.4
High School Level	54	22
Higher Secondary Level	63	25.2
Dropouts	20	8

According to our study, 40 per cent of the families have an annual income of less than ₹30,000 as a result of the imprisonment of the parent. It ultimately affects the children, and their basic needs are unattended. Many children complete their school education but for them, higher education at the college level remains a distant dream due to financial constraints. We found it difficult to locate these families at their given addresses accessed from the secondary date. Most of the families have relocated after being subjected to stigmatization and due to the post-traumatic condition of the children upon the arrest and imprisonment of their parents. The villagers hesitated to help us in reaching out to these families due to the fear of dispute.

Table 3: Family Income (Per Annum in Rupees)

Below 30,000	59	40.6
30,001–35,000	37	25.5
35,001–40,000	25	17.2
40,001–45,000	12	8.2
45,001–50,000	8	5.5
Above 50,000	4	2.7

Table 4: Occupations of the caregivers

House Maid	9	6.2
Agricultural Coolie	22	15
Beedi rolling workers	41	28.2
Tailors	11	7.5
Self-employed	16	11
Mason helpers	19	13
Fire industry workers	27	18.6

Highlights of the Findings

- Almost 90 per cent of the children with imprisoned parents or caregivers have only their mothers to serve as the sole earning member of the family, most often with no regular income. As a result, they are unable to secure even two square meals per day for their children.
- The contact between the children and their imprisoned parent or caregiver is often not possible for various reasons,

including the fact that the children would have to take leave from school in order to meet their imprisoned parent/caregiver. Also, presently, prisons do not allow interviews on Sundays.

- Even when the children meet their imprisoned parent/caregiver, in most cases, they cannot touch their parents, give them a hug or a kiss and exchange words with their wards, which is necessary – not only for the child, but also the imprisoned person. This is due to the absence of child-friendly interview halls in prisons.
- In most cases, persons in prisons did not have visitors from their families or the opportunity of their children visiting them. This has a huge toll on the mental health and well-being of the person living in incarceration.
- Although every prison in the state includes the position of a psychologist or social case worker, two counsellors and one welfare officer, in reality, most of these positions remain vacant due to non-appointment. And in all the cases where an appointment is made, these officials occupying these positions perform duties which are not directly related to the needs of the imprisoned persons, their well-being and their connection to their families.
- In a few cases, the incarcerated persons were totally unaware of the details and the location of their children since the mother herself had been murdered.
- The study has further revealed that there was no record of the distribution of the victim compensation fund to the actual victims of the crime within a stipulated time.
- The children who live in prison along with their mothers have largely been found lacking in access to regular nutritious food, snacks, milk and a pediatrician's periodic care to monitor their physical and mental growth. These children did not have a crèche with child-friendly accessories and

thus were in the midst of other women, who often did not value their childhood in the conversations to which they were party.

- Most mothers in prisons were not found to be engaged in work, which could bring them remuneration/compensation when they availed of leave facilities.
- In several cases, exclusive telephone facilities for parents to communicate with their children or vice versa were even available in male prisons and special prisons for women.

Statutes on Children's Rights

We also looked at various standards and institutions that have been developed at the national level catering to the responsibility of the State for the welfare of children.

The national standards are:

Constitution of India

- Article 14 provides that the State shall not deny to any person equality before the law or the equal protections of the laws within the territory of India.
- Article 15(3) provides that nothing in this Article shall prevent the State from making any special provision for women and children.
- Article 21 provides that no person shall be deprived of his life or personal liberty except according to procedure established by law.
- Article 21A provides that the State shall provide free and compulsory education to all children of the ages of six to fourteen years in such manner as the State may, by law, determine.
- Article 23(1) provides that traffic in human being and beggar and other similar forms of forced labour are prohibited,

and any contravention of this provision shall be an offence punishable in accordance with law.

- Article 24 provides that no child below the age of fourteen years shall be employed to work in any factory or mine or engaged in any other hazardous employment.
- Article 29(2) provides that no citizen shall be denied admission into any educational institution maintained by the State or receiving aid out of State funds on grounds only of religion, race, caste, language or any of them.
- Article 39(e) provides that the State shall, in particular, direct its policy towards securing that the health and strength of workers, men and women, and the tender age of children are not abused and that citizens are not forced by economic necessity to enter vocations unsuited to their age or strength.
- Article 39(f) provides that the State shall, in particular, direct its policy towards securing that children are given opportunities and facilities to develop in a healthy manner and in conditions of freedom and dignity, and that childhood and youth are protected against exploitation and against moral and material abandonment.
- Article 45 provides that the State shall endeavour to provide early childhood care and education for all children until they complete the age of six years.
- Article 47 provides that the State shall regard the raising of the level of nutrition and the standard of living of its people and the improvement of public health as among its primary duties.
- Article 51A(k) provides that it shall be the duty of every citizen of India who is a parent or guardian to provide opportunities for education to his child or, as the case may be, ward between the ages of six and fourteen years.

National Policy for Children, 1974

This is a policy committed to provide services to children for their physical, mental and social development.[2]

National Expert Committee on Women Prisoners, 1988

The committee, led by Justice V. R. Krishna Iyer, has devoted a section to the children of prisoners and refers to the Supreme Court's direction in *Hussinara Khatoon and Others vs State of Bihar*, which emphasizes that it is the duty of the government in social welfare to protect women and children who are homeless and destitute.

National Plan of Action for Children, 2005

Under this plan, the Ministry of Women and Child Development of the Government of India refers to special provisions for the protection of children in especially difficult circumstances, such as the children of prisoners. It is divided into four sections and all the categories of rights apply to all age groups, including before birth: child survival, child development, child protection and child participation.

The guiding principles of the National Plan of Action for Children, 2005, are:

- To regard the child as an asset and a person with human rights.
- To address issues of discrimination emanating from biases of gender, class, caste, race, religion and legal status in order to ensure equality.
- To accord utmost priority to the most disadvantaged, poorest of the poor and the least served child in all policy and programmatic interventions.

---

[2] 'Childline India'. Available: https://www.childlineindia.org.in/CP-CR Downloads/national_policy_for_children.pdf.

- To recognize the diverse stages and settings of childhood, and address the needs of each, providing to all children the entitlements that fulfil their rights and meet their needs in each situation.

The Plan has identified twelve key areas, keeping in mind the priorities and intensity of the challenges that require utmost and sustained attention in terms of outreach, programme interventions and resource allocation, so as to achieve the necessary targets and ensure the rights and entitlements of children at each stage of childhood, one of which is 'addressing and upholding the rights of Children in Difficult Circumstances'.[3]

National Policy for Children, 2013

This National Policy reaffirms that every child is unique and a supremely important national asset; that special measures and affirmative actions are required to diminish or eliminate conditions that cause discrimination; that all children have the right to grow in a family environment, in an atmosphere of happiness, love and understanding; that families are to be supported by a strong social safety net in caring for and nurturing their children. It reinforces that every child has universal inalienable and indivisible human rights. The rights of children are interrelated and inter-dependent and the best interest of the child is a primary concern in a decision and action affecting the child. According to the policy, the undeniable rights of every child and its key priorities are survival, health, nutrition, development, education, protection and participation.[4]

National Plan of Action for Children, 2016

Entitled 'Safe Children – Happy Childhood', this plan of action is based on the National Policy for Children, 2013,

---

[3] 'Childline India'.

[4] 'Childline India'.

and emphasizes four key priorities, namely survival, health and nutrition, education and development, protection and participation.

NALSA (Child Friendly Legal Services to Children and their Protection) Scheme, 2015

Its objectives are to:

- Outline the basic rights and benefits that should be afforded to children.
- Ensure legal representation to the children in need of care and protection and children in conflict with the law at all levels.
- To strengthen legal services, institutional care, counselling and support services at the national, state, district and taluk levels.
- To create an environment in the juvenile justice system, in which children are valued, encouraged and affirmed and have their rights respected and are treated as individuals.
- To ensure that mandatory authorities and institutions, like JJBs, CWCs, other welfare committees, observation and shelter homes, psychiatric hospitals or psychiatric nursing homes, commissions, boards, offices of probation officers etc have been set up under various child-friendly legislations.

Its key principles are:

- *The best interest of the child:* Every child has the right to have his or her best interests given primary consideration while providing legal services to the children in need of care and protection and children in conflict with law.
- *Welfare of the child:* The welfare of children must always come first, regardless of all other considerations. Early intervention and support should be available to promote the welfare of the child.

- *Right to dignity:* Every child has the right to be treated with dignity and compassion and their worth is to be respected and protected.
- *Right to equality and no discrimination:* A child shall be treated without discrimination of any kind, irrespective of the child's caste, race, religion, beliefs, age, family status, culture, language, ethnicity, disabilities (if any) or place of birth.
- *Principle of the right to be heard:* Every child has the right to be informed, right to be heard and to express views and concerns freely.
- *Principle of right to safety:* Every child has the right to safety at all stages and he or she shall not be subjected to any harm, abuse or neglect etc.
- *Principle of confidentiality:* The privacy of a child shall be protected by legal services institutions at all levels.[5]

National Initiative for Child Protection

Launched under the Department of Social Justice and Empowerment of the Government of India, this initiative aimed to create awareness about the United Nations Convention of the Rights of the Child and ensure that every child would have the right to safe and secure childhood.[6]

Juvenile Justice (Care and Protection) Act, 2015

This legislation provides for the care and rehabilitation of neglected children under a child welfare committee constituted in every district and provides for foster care, guardianship, adoption or institutionalization of neglected children. The said

---

[5] 'Child-friendly Legal Services'. Available: https://nalsa.gov.in/sites/default/files/document/Child%20Friendly%20Legal%20Services%20to%20Children%20and%20their%20Protection.pdf .

[6] 'Childline India'.

Act paves the way for children's homes to be set-up both by the State as well as NGOs to house the children.[7]

Integrated Child Protection Scheme

The above scheme has been launched under the Ministry of Women and Child Development by Government of India for the care and protection of neglected children in the country.[8]

Recommendations for the Well-being of the Children with Imprisoned Parents

The study revealed that parental and caregiver imprisonment affects different aspects of a child's life, including emotional and behavioural well-being, family stability and financial circumstances.

In most cases, we discovered that the regular growth of the child, his/her quality of education, health status and general well-being almost come to an end with the imprisonment of the parent/caregiver.

Only extensive studies that are yet to be undertaken will make clear whether the children of imprisoned parents are more likely to be imprisoned themselves as adults because of a lack of family, family attention and parental care.

Further studies would also indicate the impact of such imprisonment on the mental health of the child, leading him or her to choose future paths in life that they would never have done had their parents been with them, in spite of their poverty.

In this study, we have tried to ensure there are no special financial requirements that are envisaged for the commencement of the immediate implementation of the same. This study does not propose any new mechanisms, institutions or personnel.

[7] Juvenile Justice (Care and Protection of Children) Act, 2015. Available: http://cara.nic.in/PDF/JJ%20act%202015.pdf.

[8] 'Childline India'.

Perhaps the only assurance required is the appointment of an extra senior full-time staff member at all District Legal Services Authorities (DLSAs) wherein central prisons and special prisons for women are located – in Chennai, Vellore, Cuddalore, Salem, Coimbatore, Tiruchirappalli, Madurai and Palayamkottai. In addition, we seek better coordination between existing arms of the Criminal Justice Administration and its related institutions, namely the Investigation Wing, the Prosecution, the Judiciary, the Prisons Department, the Legal Services Authority with the Education Department on the one hand and the Department of Social Defence on the other, and good, effective, sensitive and competent NGOs.

A careful, creative and professional coordination of all these departments, programmes and mechanisms can thus ensure that the child of an imprisoned parent or caregiver is afforded the same care as that of a normal child. This exercise will attempt to bring meaning to Articles 14 and 15 of the Constitution.

Institutions Identified for 'Partnership' in this Study

The term employed herein is 'partnership'. This report identifies that the welfare of these 'invisible' children is the responsibility of the State. They are the central focus of this report as reflected in various national and international instruments, including those to which India is a signatory. The institutions are:

Tamil Nadu State Legal Services Authority

The National Legal Services Authority Act 1987 has created the National Legal Services Authority (NLSA), the State Legal Services Authority (SLSA), the District Legal Services Authority (DLSA) and the Taluk Legal Services Committee. The three institutions serve persons in need of free legal aid, who are undergoing incarceration in addition to their other objectives under the said act. The main implementing focus, however, would be the DLSA headed by a Member Secretary, who is a Judicial Officer of the rank of a Sub Judge in the state of Tamil Nadu. The DLSA is contemplated to be the coordinator of the scheme under whose most effective coordination the entire scheme will revolve. Of course, this has to have the full collaboration of all the other departments and units.

District Child Protection Unit (DCPU)

The District Child Protection Unit constituted under the Integrated Child Protection Scheme (ICPS) 22 has been given the responsibility to create a district-level system that efficiently and effectively protects children, based on the cardinal principles of protection of child rights and the best interest of the child. The ICPS has a special objective to contribute to the well-being of children in difficult circumstances – in our case, the children of incarcerated parents – as well as to ensure reduction of their vulnerability in situations and actions that lead to their abuse, neglect, exploitation, stigmatization, abandonment and, most importantly, their separation from families and their sufferings that are untold stories. Their miseries are invisible to courts, their hardships are hidden within the larger society. We want to recommend measures to provide visibility to the invisible.

The DCPU has in its list of varied functions, in accordance with the ICPS:

- Ensure that for each child in need of care, there is an individual care plan which is regularly reviewed.
- Identify families at risk and children in need of care and protection through effective networking and linkages.
- Assess the number of children in difficult circumstances and create district-specific databases to monitor trends and patterns of children in difficult circumstances.
- Support implementation of family-based, non-institutional services, including sponsorship, foster care, adoption and aftercare.

- Ensure setting up of district, block and village-level child protection committees for effective implementation of the Child Protection Scheme.

These are but a few of their many functions. The DCPU has a District Child Protection Officer (DCPO) working directly under the district collector, a protection officer looking after institutional care, a counsellor, a social worker, an outreach worker and community volunteers. In addition, the DCPU also has a legal-cum-probation officer assisted by a counsellor, social worker, outreach worker and community volunteers.

Thus, at the district level, the DCPU is a well-equipped institutional mechanism, which caters to the needs of children in difficult circumstances. Every DCPU has a recurring annual expenditure of ₹23 lakhs towards staff salaries and a district sponsorship and foster care fund of ₹10 lakhs.

Juvenile Justice (Care and Protection of Children) Act, 2015

The JJ Act, 2015, mandates the establishment of a Child Welfare Committee (CWC) in each district as the final authority to dispose of cases for the care, protection, treatment, development and rehabilitation of children in need of care and protection and provide for their basic needs and protection of human rights. The JJ Act mandates the establishment of a variety of institutions, working to open shelters under Section 43, the aftercare of children leaving childcare institutions under Section 46, special homes under Section 48, children's homes under Section 50 and fit facilities under Section 51.

Thus, the JJ Act envisages the establishment of Special Institutions for Child Care run by the government in every district. These institutions can cater to the need of children of incarcerated parents when non-institutional care is ruled out. All these institutions are under the direct supervision of the District CWC.

Chief Education Officer (CEO) of the School Education Department

The Right of Children to Free and Compulsory Education Act, 2009 (RTE Act) 26 provides for free and compulsory education to at least 25 per cent of the students in class one who belong to weaker sections and disadvantaged groups in the neighbourhood, and further provide a compulsory elementary education until its completion – up to class eight as of now. This is a statutory mandate to be carried out in all unaided schools, which do not receive any aids or grants from the appropriate government to meet their expenses. This provision can be used to prevail upon private schools to ensure quality education, explaining to them the special circumstances of the children of incarcerated parents, who will clearly fall under this category and get them admitted to such schools free of cost.

Non-governmental Organizations (NGOs)

There are very few reputable NGOs that assist prisoners and their families. Some of them are based within the district while some others, such as the Prison Ministry of India (PMI), are known to function at the state and national levels. In the scheme that we proposed, we did not venture into the efforts of NGOs and restricted our recommendations to statutory and government programmes.

Private Educational Institutions

We also propose that esteemed private educational institutions provide opportunities for the students to pursue higher education. They have excellent facilities on a par with international standards but also intend to offer seats to the deserving students from below-the-poverty-line backgrounds. Opportunities should be made available for deserving students from this category so they can study at esteemed educational institutions like the SRM Group of institutions, Sathyabama institutes and so on.

Conclusion

In his thought 'hate the crime and not the criminal', Mahatma Gandhi pointed out that we cannot allow children to be abandoned and exposed to hatred because their parents are imprisoned. The nurturing and solicitude of these children are our collective responsibility. The programme should find a prominent place in any national plan for the development of human resources, so that the children grow up to become robust citizens, physically fit, mentally alert and morally healthy, endowed with all the necessary skills and motivations. Our aim should be to provide equal opportunities for development to all children, which would serve our larger purpose of reducing inequality and ensuring social justice.

NOTES ON THE CONTRIBUTORS

Amrita Paul works as Senior Programme Officer at the prison reforms programme (Access to Justice) of the Commonwealth Human Rights Initiative. She studied at National Law University, Jodhpur, and the National Law School of India University, Bangalore. At CHRI, she has been associated with the initiatives on access to information as well as to justice. Her work revolves around measures to reduce prolonged detention, prevent unnecessary detentions and ensure access to effective legal aid for persons in custody, especially refugees and foreign nationals. Along with research and advocacy, she works closely with the institutions of the State to devise and implement workable solutions.

Chaman Lal belongs to the Madhya Pradesh cadre of the Indian Police Service (IPS), 1964. Besides serving in various ranks in his parent cadre, he has served on deputation to the BSF, ITBP, SPG, Punjab Police, Nagaland Police and the Shah Commission of Inquiry, which looked into the excesses of the Emergency. After retiring, he has served as Special Rapporteur on pro-bono basis in the National Human Rights Commission for nearly eleven years on human rights matters relating to jails, child labour, bonded labour, mental healthcare, poverty alleviation programmes and tribal issues.

He is a recipient of the Police Medal for Meritorious Services, the President's Police Medal for Distinguished Services and the Padma Shri. He is the only police officer of the country to be honoured with the Nani Palkhivala Award for Civil Liberties.

Deepan Kumar Sarkar is an advocate at the High Court of Calcutta where he works on constitutional, company and other commercial and civil matters as well as criminal and preventive detention matters. Along with Samaraditya Pal, he co-authored the multi-volume treatise, *India's Constitution: Origins and Evolution* (LexisNexis, 2014–19).

He has been associated with the prison reforms programme of the CHRI since 2010 as Retainer. He is also a guest faculty at the Administrative Training Institute, Kolkata, the training institute for government servants and at RICA, Kolkata, the training institute for jail officers.

K. R. Raja graduated with a master's degree in social work and a specialization in medical psychiatry at the Pondicherry Central University. Along with a master's degree in criminology and police administration from Manonmanian Sundaranar University, Tirunelveli, he also holds a law degree from Government Law College, Madurai.

He has worked on social work principles to redress problems among people with HIV/AIDS and psychiatric illness, destitute, intellectually challenged children, abandoned elderly citizens, victims of organ trafficking, and prisoners and their children. He has volunteered and worked with Prisoners Assistance Nepal, an NGO in Kathmandu, and helped in children's home management. He was awarded a one-year fellowship for social entrepreneurs by Kanthari International Institute of Social Entrepreneurs.

Madan B. Lokur is a former judge of the Supreme Court of India and, presently, a judge at the Supreme Court of Fiji. He was appointed as Additional Solicitor General of India in 1998 and a judge of the Delhi High Court in February 1999. He was the Chief Justice of the Gauhati High Court and Chief Justice of the High Court of Andhra Pradesh.

During his time in the Supreme Court, he made suggestions for improvements in the working of the homes and organizations under the Juvenile Justice Act, was a member and later chairperson of the mediation and conciliation project committee of the Supreme Court; the judge in charge of the E-committee of the Supreme Court; and the executive chairman of the Supreme Court Legal Services Committee and the National Legal Services Authority (NALSA).

Sabika Abbas is a programme officer with the prison reforms programme at the CHRI. She has been working on criminal justice reforms in India for more than six years.

Abbas was previously a criminal justice fellow for two years at the Tata Institute of Social Sciences (TISS), Mumbai. As a fellow, she worked on access to socio-legal aid and guidance with the inmates of the Aligarh district prison. At the CHRI, Abbas has engaged in prison monitoring and policy-level advocacy across different states of the country.

Sangeeta Barooah Pisharoty is a Delhi-based journalist and writer from Assam. She is currently National Affairs Editor of *The Wire* where she writes on culture, politics, and the Northeast. She began her foray into journalism working at the United News of India (UNI), where she was the first woman from the Northeast in the New Delhi office. In 2011, she won the Inclusive Media Fellowship of the Centre for the Study of Developing Societies (CSDS) for a series on the loss of livelihood due to annual erosion in Assam's Majuli island, in the

Brahmaputra river. In 2017, she received the Ramnath Goenka Excellence in Journalism Award for feature writing.

S. Ramakrishnan has over thirty-four years of experience in the Indian Police Service, during which time he successfully led diverse teams and worked with the West Bengal Police, Calcutta Police as well as organizations such as the S. V. P. National Police Academy, Hyderabad and the Border Security Force.

He is the founder–director of the Regional Institute of Correctional Administration (RICA), Kolkata. He also compiled the revised draft of the West Bengal Jail Code. He served as a consultant on Police Training with the UNICEF and was associated in the development of awareness courses for the Child Welfare Officers in the state police.

He has been awarded the Police Medal for meritorious services and the President's Medal for distinguished service.

Sugandha Shankar is a Senior Programme Officer in the prison reforms programme at the CHRI. An ardent advocate for prisoners' rights, she has worked extensively on prison oversight, undertrial review committees, legal aid reform and pre-trial detention issues for over a decade in India. She has authored various reports, developed training material and trained functionaries, including paralegals and lawyers.

Shankar is a law graduate and holds a diploma in human rights and law, and a bachelor's degree in political science from Sri Venkateswara College, University of Delhi.

Sunetra Choudhury is a Delhi-based journalist working in television and print for the last two decades. She is currently the National Political Editor of the *Hindustan Times*. Using her reporting as an inspiration for her writing, Sunetra has written *Behind Bars: Prison Tales of India's Most Famous* (Roli, 2017). In 2009, she wrote a political travelogue called *Braking*

News (Hachette, 2010). Her latest book, *Black Warrant* (2019), co-authored with Sunil Gupta, recollects his time as the jailer and legal officer of Tihar Jail.

Vrinda Grover is a lawyer, researcher and human rights activist based in New Delhi. She obtained her law degree from Delhi University and her master's degree in law from New York University, School of Law. As a lawyer, she specializes in constitutional law, criminal law and human rights and played a key role in the campaign for amending criminal laws relating to sexual violence against women, which led to the passing of the Criminal Law Amendment Act, 2013.

In 2018, she was conferred an honorary degree by the SOAS University of London, for her contribution to human rights and civil liberties issues. In 2013, the *Time* magazine listed her among the 100 most influential people in the world.

ACKNOWLEDGEMENTS

Grateful acknowledgement is made to these copyright holders for permission to reprint copyrighted material in this volume.

'Wahid and the Different Shades of Torture', extract from *Behind Bars: Prison Tales of India's Most Famous* by Sunetra Choudhury, published by Roli Books, 2017, copyright © Sunetra Choudhury 2017, reprinted by permission of the author and the publisher.

'Life in Detention Centres', extract from *Assam: The Accord, the Discord* by Sangeeta Barooah Pisharoty, published by Penguin Random House India, 2019, copyright © Sangeeta Barooah Pisharoty 2019, reprinted by permission of the author and the publisher.

The editors of the volume also want to thank Poornima Gusain, CHRI, for her assistance in putting together this publication.